Guidance notes for the

Term Service Contract

This contract should be used for the appointment of a supplier for a period of time to manage and provide a service

An NEC document

April 2013

Construction Clients' Board endorsement of NEC3

The Construction Clients' Board recommends that public sector organisations use the NEC3 contracts when procuring construction. Standardising use of this comprehensive suite of contracts should help to deliver efficiencies across the public sector and promote behaviours in line with the principles of *Achieving Excellence in Construction.*

Facilities Management Board support for NEC3

The Facilities Management Board recognises that the NEC Term Service Contracts support good practice in FM Procurement in the public sector.

Cabinet Office UK

supported by
ADVANCING OUR PROFESSION

BIFM recommends the use of NEC3 Term Service Contract and NEC3 Term Service Short Contract for all types of Facilities Management and maintenance contracts.

NEC is a division of Thomas Telford Ltd, which is a wholly owned subsidiary of the Institution of Civil Engineers (ICE), the owner and developer of the NEC.

The NEC is a family of standard contracts, each of which has these characteristics:

- Its use stimulates good management of the relationship between the two parties to the contract and, hence, of the work included in the contract.
- It can be used in a wide variety of commercial situations, for a wide variety of types of work and in any location.
- It is a clear and simple document – using language and a structure which are straightforward and easily understood.

NEC3 Term Service Contract is one of the NEC family and is consistent with all other NEC3 documents. This document comprises the Term Service Contract Guidance Notes. Also available are the Term Service Contract Flow Charts.

ISBN (complete box set) 978 0 7277 5867 5
ISBN (this document) 978 0 7277 5921 4
ISBN (Term Service Contract Flow Charts) 978 0 7277 5923 8
ISBN (how to write the TSC Service Information) 978 0 7277 5925 2
ISBN (how to use the TSC communication forms) 978 0 7277 5927 6

First edition June 2005
Reprinted with amendments 2007
Reprinted 2010 (twice), 2012
Reprinted with amendments 2013

British Library Cataloguing in Publication Data for this publication is available from the British Library.

Typeset by Academic + Technical, Bristol

Printed and bound in Great Britain by Bell & Bain Limited, Glasgow, UK

CONTENTS

FOREWORD

I was delighted to be asked to write the Foreword for the NEC3 Contracts.

I have followed the outstanding rise and success of NEC contracts for a number of years now, in particular during my tenure as the 146th President of the Institution of Civil Engineers, 2010/11.

In my position as UK Government's Chief Construction Adviser, I am working with Government and industry to ensure Britain's construction sector is equipped with the knowledge, skills and best practice it needs in its transition to a low carbon economy. I am promoting innovation in the sector, including in particular the use of Building Information Modelling (BIM) in public sector construction procurement; and the synergy and fit with the collaborative nature of NEC contracts is obvious. The Government's construction strategy is a very significant investment and NEC contracts will play an important role in setting high standards of contract preparation, management and the desirable behaviour of our industry.

In the UK, we are faced with having to deliver a 15–20 per cent reduction in the cost to the public sector of construction during the lifetime of this Parliament. Shifting mind-set, attitude and behaviour into best practice NEC processes will go a considerable way to achieving this.

Of course, NEC contracts are used successfully around the world in both public and private sector projects; this trend seems set to continue at an increasing pace. NEC contracts are, according to my good friend and NEC's creator Dr Martin Barnes CBE, about better management of projects. This is quite achievable and I encourage you to understand NEC contracts to the best you can and exploit the potential this offers us all.

Peter Hansford

UK Government's Chief Construction Adviser
Cabinet Office

PREFACE

The NEC contracts are the only suite of standard contracts designed to facilitate and encourage good management of the projects on which they are used. The experience of using NEC contracts around the world is that they really make a difference. Previously, standard contracts were written mainly as legal documents best left in the desk drawer until costly and delaying problems had occurred and there were lengthy arguments about who was to blame.

The language of NEC contracts is clear and simple, and the procedures set out are all designed to stimulate good management. Foresighted collaboration between all the contributors to the project is the aim. The contracts set out how the interfaces between all the organisations involved will be managed – from the client through the designers and main contractors to all the many subcontractors and suppliers.

Versions of the NEC contract are specific to the work of professional service providers such as project managers and designers, to main contractors, to subcontractors and to suppliers. The wide range of situations covered by the contracts means that they do not need to be altered to suit any particular situation.

The NEC contracts are the first to deal specifically and effectively with management of the inevitable risks and uncertainties which are encountered to some extent on all projects. Management of the expected is easy, effective management of the unexpected draws fully on the collaborative approach inherent in the NEC contracts.

Most people working on projects using the NEC contracts for the first time are hugely impressed by the difference between the confrontational characteristics of traditional contracts and the teamwork engendered by the NEC. The NEC does not include specific provisions for dispute avoidance. They are not necessary. Collaborative management itself is designed to avoid disputes and it really works.

It is common for the final account for the work on a project to be settled at the time when the work is finished. The traditional long period of expensive professional work after completion to settle final payments just is not needed.

The NEC contracts are truly a massive change for the better for the industries in which they are used.

Dr Martin Barnes CBE

Originator of the NEC contracts

ACKNOWLEDGEMENTS

The first edition of the NEC3 Term Service Contract was drafted by the Institution of Civil Engineers NEC Panel working through the Term Service Contract Working Group whose members were:

P. A. Baird, BSc, CEng, FICE, M(SA)ICE, MAPM
M. Barnes, BSc(Eng), PhD, FREng, FICE, FCIOB, CCMI, ACIArb, MBCS, FInstCES, FAPM
T. W. Weddell, BSc, CEng, DIC, FICE, FIStructE, ACIArb

The Flow Charts were produced by Ross Hayes with assistance from Tom Nicholson.

The NEC3 Term Service Contract Guidance Notes were produced by the Institution of Civil Engineers and were mainly drafted by Bill Weddell with the assistance of Dr Martin Barnes and P. A. Baird.

The original NEC was designed and drafted by Dr Martin Barnes then of Coopers and Lybrand with the assistance of Professor J. G. Perry then of the University of Birmingham, T. W. Weddell then of Travers Morgan Management, T. H. Nicholson, Consultant to the Institution of Civil Engineers, A. Norman then of the University of Manchester Institute of Science and Technology and P. A. Baird, then Corporate Contracts Consultant, Eskom, South Africa.

The members of the NEC Panel are:

P. Higgins, BSc, CEng, FICE, FCIArb (Chairman)
P. A. Baird, BSc, CEng, FICE, M(SA)ICE, MAPM
M. Barnes, BSc(Eng), PhD, FREng, FICE, FCIOB, CCMI, ACIArb, MBCS, FInstCES, FAPM
A. J. Bates, FRICS, MInstCES
A. J. M. Blackler, BA, LLB(Cantab), MCIArb
P. T. Cousins, BEng(Tech), DipArb, CEng, MICE, MCIArb, MCMI
L. T. Eames, BSc, FRICS, FCIOB
F. Forward, BA(Hons), DipArch, MSc(Const Law), RIBA, FCIArb
Professor J. G. Perry, MEng, PhD, CEng, FICE, MAPM
N. C. Shaw, FCIPS, CEng, MIMechE
T. W. Weddell, BSc, CEng, DIC, FICE, FIStructE, ACIArb

NEC Consultant:

R. A. Gerrard, BSc(Hons), MRICS, FCIArb, FCInstCES

Secretariat:

A. Cole, LLB, LLM, BL
J. M. Hawkins, BA(Hons), MSc
F. N. Vernon (Technical Adviser), BSc, CEng, MICE

AMENDMENTS

Full details of all amendments are available on www.neccontract.com.

CHAPTER 1   THE NEC FAMILY OF CONTRACTS

The NEC system of contracting was developed as a result of much dissatisfaction in the construction industry. Many in the industry felt that the legal terms under which projects were carried out (the standard conditions of contract) had not kept pace with developments in technology and management. For about 120 years, dating from the railway era of the 19th century, the way in which public works were designed and built remained largely stagnant. Increasingly it was felt that application of legal conditions appropriate to the 19th century to projects in the late 20th century was producing problems which did not serve the interests of either promoters or contractors. These problems included complaints by Employers (promoters) of frequent increases in the cost of projects, often with little prior notice, delays in completion and frequent disputes which were resolved only by expensive arbitration and litigation.

'A fundamental review'

Thus in 1985 the Institution of Civil Engineers (ICE) decided 'to lead a fundamental review of alternative contract strategies for civil engineering design and construction with the objective of identifying the need for good practice'. After much discussion and consultation, this review resulted in the publication in 1991 of a consultative edition, and in 1993 of the first edition of the New Engineering Contract (NEC). Since then, in response to industry demands, further standard forms of contract have been produced, using the same principles as were used in the NEC first edition.

The Latham Report

In 1994, Sir Michael Latham produced his report *Constructing the Team*. This report was commissioned by the UK Government in collaboration with the construction industry and its professions. It recommended that the NEC should be adopted by clients in both the private and public sectors and suggested that it should become the national standard contract across the whole of engineering and construction work generally. As a result of certain recommendations in the Latham Report and further consultation, a second edition (renamed the Engineering and Construction Contract – ECC) was published in 1995.

Increasing use of the NEC contracts

The ECC represented a radical change from the traditional ways in which construction work was carried out and Employers were understandably apprehensive about changing to such a different system. However, as the benefits of the new approach came to be understood and experienced in practice, the ECC became increasingly accepted. Employers appreciated how changes could be properly managed, and how costs and time delays could be controlled by effective project management procedures. Its use gradually spread to all sectors of the construction industry – building, mechanical and electrical engineering, process engineering as well as civil engineering. As it was designed also for international use, it began to be used in countries other than the UK. It is now used in over 20 different countries and translation into other languages is progressing. A Chinese version was produced in 2001.

NEC3 contracts

The current list of published NEC3 contracts is stated below:

- NEC3 Engineering and Construction Contract (ECC)
- NEC3 Engineering and Construction Subcontract (ECS)
- NEC3 Engineering and Construction Short Contract (ECSC)
- NEC3 Engineering and Construction Short Subcontract (ECSS)
- NEC3 Professional Services Contract (PSC)
- NEC3 Professional Services Short Contract (PSSC)
- NEC3 Term Service Contract (TSC)
- NEC3 Term Service Short Contract (TSSC)
- NEC3 Supply Contract (SC)
- NEC3 Supply Short Contract (SSC)
- NEC3 Framework Contract (FC)
- NEC3 Adjudicator's Contract (AC)

For general guidance on when to use each contract refer to the NEC3 Procurement and Contract Strategies guide, available on www.neccontract.com.

Culture change

The period following the publication of the first edition of the NEC has been a time of change of culture in the construction industry. Many problems were traced to the traditional method of procurement, which was to invite tenders from a number of contractors and select the lowest. This did not always represent best value for the Employer. The benefits of longer-term arrangements between Employer and Contractor began to be appreciated. These took the form of partnering and framework agreements, which made possible continuous improvement. Sir John Egan's Report *Rethinking Construction* (1998) did much to accelerate the change. The NEC system is a vital part of the culture change in that its terms are entirely consistent with the new principles – fundamentally a change from confrontation to co-operation and collaboration between the parties.

Have the NEC contracts been successful?

In the early years of the NEC, it was not easy to prove the success of the NEC contracts since this can only be done over a period of time to enable results to be compared and contrasted with projects using traditional contracts. However, a number of cases have been documented. These, together with the feedback from all parties involved, indicate that the benefits are considerable. Almost all Employers who have tried one of the NEC contracts have decided to continue to use it as a matter of policy.

CHAPTER 2   KEY PRINCIPLES OF THE NEC CONTRACTS

The NEC was drafted with three main objectives

- flexibility
- clarity
- stimulus to good management.

These principles have been used also in drafting the later contracts. The success of the NEC contracts indicates that these objectives have been achieved.

Flexibility

It was felt that one of the problems with the traditional standard conditions of contract was that there was no simple mechanism to adapt them to the particular circumstances of individual projects. The result was that they were sometimes used in situations for which they were not suited. Thus the NEC was designed for

- use with the different construction disciplines,
- varying amounts of design by the contractor,
- different methods of pricing and payment,
- appropriate allocation of risk and
- international use.

Clarity

One of the problems with the traditional forms is that the average user finds them difficult to understand. Hence NEC drafting was based on the assumption that the contract should be user-friendly and clear. This has been achieved by using short sentences, bullet points and the avoidance of unnecessary legal terms without compromising legal robustness. Subjective terms – so often the cause of disputes – have been avoided as far as possible.

Stimulus to good management

This is one of the most important characteristics of the NEC contracts. It is founded on the proposition that foresighted co-operative management of the interactions between the parties can shrink the risks inherent in construction work. Development in project management techniques has progressed faster than the evolution of forms of contract. Thus the contract includes not only the obligations of the parties but also contractually binding management procedures when various situations arise. Thus the different parties are able to contribute to the management of a project by improved practices. The parties are motivated by means of the contract to apply such practices to their work.

There are two principles on which the NEC contracts are based and which impact upon the objective of stimulating good management.

- Foresight applied collaboratively mitigates problems and shrinks risk.
- Clear division of function and responsibility helps accountability and motivates people to play their part.

Risk is a major element in construction contracts and its importance is being increasingly recognised. The NEC contracts allocate clearly these risks between the parties. However, their main task is to reduce the incidence of the risks by application of collaborative foresight. In this way, they aim to improve the outcome of the projects generally for parties whose interests might seem to be opposed.

Prominent examples of the management procedures are the early warning procedure, the Contractor's programme (the *Contractor's* Plan in the Term Service Contract) and the way in which compensation events are dealt with. Compensation events are events which may lead to a change in payment to the Contractor or the timing or both. Generally, valuation of compensation events is based on a forecast of the impact of the event upon the Contractor's costs. Different ways of dealing with the problem may be considered by assessing alternatives. Changes to payment are based upon a quotation. Once the quotation is agreed, the Contractor carries the risk of the forecast of cost impact (except for the cost reimbursement contracts). This arrangement should stimulate foresight, to enable the Employer to make rational decisions about changes to the work with reasonable certainty of cost and time implications.

The ECC makes important use of the programme for design construction and installation. The requirement of an up-to-date and realistic programme maintained by the Contractor is used in joint decision-making between the Contractor and the Project Manager. Similar requirements in the Term Service Contract in relation to the Contractor's plan facilitate decision-making between the Contractor and the Service Manager.

CHAPTER 3   INTRODUCTION TO THE TERM SERVICE CONTRACT

There are some published standard forms of maintenance-type contracts, but these are similar in nature to traditional forms of construction contracts. Generally, they suffer from the same disadvantages and frequently result in similar problems. Some organisations have used bespoke maintenance contracts for many years. Many of these have been adapted from standard forms of construction contracts which have long been outdated.

As the benefits of the NEC contracts became increasingly understood and accepted in the changing environment of construction, the demand arose for a Term Service Contract based on the same principles. In response to this demand, the Institution of Civil Engineers published a consultative version in May 2002. A number of comments were received and these have been considered in producing this first edition. Updates in other NEC contracts have also been taken into consideration and relevant changes incorporated.

Purpose of guidance notes

The purpose of these guidance notes is to explain the background of the Term Service Contract (TSC), the reasons for some of its provisions and to provide guidance on how to use it. The guidance notes are not contract documents, neither are they part of the TSC. They should not be used for legal interpretation of the meaning of the TSC.

When should the TSC be used?

Although at first reading the TSC may appear to be similar to existing standard or bespoke forms of maintenance-type contracts, to rely on such an impression would be wrong. Most procedures in the TSC are based on good management practice and often differ from current practice. This is not a change for the sake of change, since the application of NEC principles in pursuit of its objectives has left very little of conventional practice to be incorporated unchanged.

Users of the TSC must, therefore, study it carefully as the words are not simply different expressions of familiar practice. The TSC is drafted in a simple and clear style, but its differences from current practice mean that some explanation and consideration of how it will work is necessary when it is first used. That is the purpose of these guidance notes. They are essential reading for those using the TSC for the first time. They will continue to be useful in training people coming into the management of service contracts in how to make best use of the TSC.

The TSC is also essentially different from other forms of contract in the NEC family of contracts. It has been designed for use in a wide variety of situations – not restricted to construction. It is essentially a contract for a Contractor to provide a service (not limited to a professional or construction service) to an Employer from a starting date and throughout a service period. It uses established NEC procedures and wording as much as possible. It is designed for managing and providing a service – not for managing a project. The service may be provided continuously over the period of the contract or on a task-by-task call-off basis.

The TSC should not be used for low risk straightforward services. In that case the Term Service Short Contract (TSSC) should be used. The service is usually provided on the Employer's premises but may not be. The service may include physical work, such as cleaning, painting or other maintenance, but may not do. In the public sector, the TSC is designed to be used for all contracted-out services, whether including a physical content or not.

Examples of its use in the construction sector may be wide ranging and include

- maintenance of highways in a particular area,
- periodic inspection of bridges and reporting,
- cleaning of streets in an urban area,
- refuse collection and disposal,
- collection and recycling of domestic waste materials,
- maintaining public parks and landscape areas,
- maintaining heating, lighting and ventilation of buildings,
- maintenance of a canal and servicing its leisure facilities,
- snow clearing of highways,
- maintaining a nuclear power station,
- providing security personnel for an installation, site or building.

Examples of other and more complex applications are

- providing ambulance services for a group of hospitals,
- servicing and maintaining airport terminal buildings,
- providing commercial television programmes in a geographic area,
- providing data processing services by a computer systems company,
- Public–Private Partnership enterprises, perhaps alongside construction projects under the ECC, e.g. the construction of a new prison and subsequent running of the prison.

It is important to appreciate that the TSC is not a contract for a project. The principle of the TSC is that contracting to maintain an existing state A for a period of time is a service. Contracting to achieve a state B when the present state is state A is not a service – it is a project. However, a modest amount of improving the condition of an asset can sensibly be included in a TSC. Maintenance for the purpose of the TSC includes renewal and replacement of things which have become worn out, and hence may include some 'betterment' of particular items.

The contract

In any particular case, the contract will consist of

a) the core clauses – these must be included in every contract.
b) one main Option, selected from three main Options

 Option A Priced contract with price list,
 Option C Target contract with price list,
 Option E Cost reimbursable contract.

(The choice of the main Option largely determines the allocation of the financial risk between Employer and Contractor and how the Contractor is to be paid for the services he provides.)

c) one of the Dispute Resolution Options,
d) the selected secondary Options, including those relating to national legislation,
e) the Price List and
f) the Contract Data, which is contract specific.

Subcontracts

The TSC has been designed on the assumption that work may be subcontracted. A standard form of subcontract has not been published but may be in the future if justified by demand. However, in Appendix 4 of these guidance notes, guidance is given on how to convert the TSC into a subcontract. This is a fairly straightforward operation and has the advantage of largely making the subcontract back-to-back with the TSC as the main contract. This leaves the Contractor with little residual risk. It also has the convenience that Contractor's and Subcontractor's staff do not have to become familiar with two different sets of text and procedure.

There is nothing to prevent a subcontract using a different main Option from that used in the main contract. For example, the main TSC contract may be carried out as a target contract under Option C, but it may be more appropriate to use Option A for the subcontract.

Because of the legal and practical problems of accountability which frequently ensue, no provision is made in the TSC for nomination of subcontractors. The principle of the TSC is that the Contractor is fully responsible for every aspect of managing the provision of the service. Alternatives to nominating subcontractors whilst achieving similar objectives are as follows.

- Making the Contractor responsible for all work. He may then subcontract parts and the Service Manager retains some control over the identity of the subcontractors provided any withholding of acceptance is for a reason stated in the contract. This is the policy followed in the TSC.
- Providing for separate contracts, with the Employer's Service Manager managing the time and physical interfaces between them.
- Including lists of acceptable subcontractors for particular tasks in the Service Information.

Where national or international law requires, the Service Information should include a statement of the award criteria for subcontracts.

Acceptance of a subcontractor cannot be withdrawn later, provided his appointment complies with the conditions of contract.

Clause numbering

The TSC is arranged in nine sections.

1 General
2 The *Contractor*'s main responsibilities
3 Time
4 Testing and Defects
5 Payment
6 Compensation events
7 Use of equipment, Plant and Materials
8 Risks and insurance
9 Termination

The first digit of a clause number, whether for a core clause or a main Option clause, is the number of the section to which the clause belongs. Where a clause is used in more than one main Option, the same number is used.

The secondary Option clauses are numbered separately and are prefixed by the Option letter.

The tables in Appendix 1 of these guidance notes illustrate the integration of the main Option clauses and clauses within the core clauses and list the secondary Option clauses.

Roles of the parties

The *Service Manager*

The Service Manager is appointed by the Employer, usually from his own staff, but may be from outside. His role within the TSC is to manage the contract for the Employer with the intention of achieving the Employer's objectives for providing the service. The TSC places considerable authority in the hands of the Service Manager. It assumes that he has the Employer's authority to carry out the actions and make the decisions which are required of him.

The contractual role of the Service Manager is defined in terms of the actions and decisions he is to take. The Service Manager is free to seek the Employer's views as much or as little as his relationship and contract with the Employer requires. He will normally maintain close contact with the Employer so that his decisions reflect the Employer's business objectives. He has authority to change the service, to instruct the Contractor and generally to apply his managerial judgement. Positive management from both sides is encouraged.

One important role of the Service Manager is to monitor the performance of the Contractor. He may check whether the performance of the Contractor is defective, and if so, ensure that the defect is corrected or payment to the Contractor adjusted to take account of the defect.

The *Adjudicator*

The Adjudicator is appointed jointly by the Employer and the Contractor for the contract. The method of selecting the Adjudicator may vary. Whichever method is chosen it is important that the person selected is acceptable to both parties and that he has the confidence of both parties. One method is for the Employer to select a number of names and require the Contractor to choose one of them. Alternatively, the Employer may invite the Contractor to propose, suitable names from which the Employer selects one.

The Adjudicator becomes involved only when a dispute is referred to him. As a person independent of both Employer and Contractor, he is required to give a decision on the dispute within stated time limits. If either party does not accept his decision, they may proceed to the tribunal (either arbitration or the courts).

The contract strategy

The Employer chooses the contract strategy for the contract. The main factors to be taken into account in deciding the type of contract to use are

- what the risks are and how they can be best managed,
- who is best placed to manage the risks,
- what total risk is tolerable for the Contractor,
- how clearly the Service Information can be defined and
- the likelihood of change in the Service Information.

The main Options offer different basic allocations of risk between the Employer and Contractor.

- Option A is a priced contract in which the risks of being able to provide the service at the agreed prices are largely borne by the Contractor.
- Option C is a target contract in which the financial risks are shared by the Employer and Contractor in an agreed proportion.
- Option E is a cost reimbursable contract in which the financial risk is largely borne by the Employer.

The referencing of the main Options has been determined by making them consistent with the main Options in other contracts in the NEC family of contracts. Hence Options B, D and F are not included since they are not appropriate or necessary for a Term Service Contract.

All the main Options can be used for various types of Service Information – both in a case where only the performance is specified (leaving the Contractor to decide how the service is to be provided) and also where the service is described in prescriptive terms.

There are ten secondary Options prefixed X, any of which may be incorporated in the contract according to particular circumstances and how it is considered that certain risks should be allocated. There are a few restrictions on use of some of the secondary Options.

There are two secondary Options prefixed Y, which relate to UK legislation.

The main Options

Option A: Priced contract with price list

The Price List is a list of activities normally prepared by the Contractor which he proposes to carry out in Providing the Service. The Price List is priced by the Contractor. It may contain lump sum items and the prices for these are paid only when the Contractor has completed the items described. It may also contain items which are described in quantitative terms. For these items, the Contractor enters a rate per unit quantity and the Contractor is paid a sum of money which is the quantity of work completed multiplied by the rate. Where the Contractor is paid per unit of time, e.g. £x per month for a particular part of the service, payment to the Contractor is based on the total time to the date of the assessment multiplied by the rate per unit of time. The Price List is priced by the Contractor, taking into account the information in the contract documents and including for all matters which are at the Contractor's risk. A pro-forma Price List is included in Appendix 6.

Option A is appropriate where the service to be provided by the Contractor can be clearly defined and the risk carried by the Contractor is relatively low. The Contractor is then able to complete the Price List and assess the rates and prices fairly precisely with reasonable confidence.

Option C: Target contract with price list

Option C is a cost reimbursable contract in which the Contractor is paid his Defined Cost together with the 'Contractor's share' using the mechanism of a 'pain/gain' share formula. The latter provides an incentive for the Contractor to minimise cost since the more he economises on cost, the greater his share. The Contractor's share is calculated by comparing the Defined Cost (broadly representing actual cost) at various stages during the provision of the service, with a target price (the Prices) which is calculated from the rates and prices in the Price List. The difference between the Prices and the Price for Services Provided to Date (PSPD) is divided into share ranges. The Contractor's share is calculated for each of the share ranges and the total of these is the total Contractor's share payable to the Contractor. If when the Contractor's share is calculated, the PSPD is greater than the Prices at that time, the Contractor pays the Employer his share of the difference.

Certain defined 'Disallowed Cost' (clause 11.2(6)) is deducted in calculating the Defined Cost to determine payments due to the Contractor. The Fee is then added to the Defined Cost. The Fee is intended to broadly cover the Contractor's head office overheads and profit. It is calculated from tendered fee percentages applied to the Defined Cost. The direct fee percentage is applied to the Defined Cost related to the Contractor's own work and the subcontracted fee percentage is applied to the Defined Cost related to subcontract work. The target (the Prices) is adjusted to allow for compensation events as they are assessed in accordance with the contract. Compensation events are events which are at the financial risk of the Employer, e.g. a Service Manager's instruction to change the services described in the Service Information.

Option C is appropriate where the anticipated Contractor's risks in providing the service are relatively high such that a priced contract under Option A could lead to many changes and possible disputes on payment. It is also appropriate where the exact nature and extent of the service to be provided is not fully defined.

Option E: Cost reimbursable contract

Under this Option, the Contractor is paid Defined Cost plus the Fee. It is therefore similar to Option C except that there is no Contractor's share and thus no financial incentive for the Contractor to minimise cost. This Option therefore represents higher financial risk to the Employer. It should be used when the definition of the service to be provided is inadequate even as a basis for estimating a target price. It may be appropriate where the Employer is anxious for the Contractor to begin providing the service but before the nature of the service can be properly specified. In such circumstances, the Contractor cannot be expected to take cost risks other than those which entail control of his employees and other resources. Under this Option, the Price List is used only for the purposes of forecasting Defined Cost and the financial outcome.

The secondary Options

The referencing of the secondary Options has been determined by making them consistent with the secondary Options in other secondary Options in the NEC family of contracts. Hence the numbering of the 'X Options' are not consecutive as some of them have not been included in the TSC.

Option W: Dispute resolution

There are two procedures included for the resolution of Dispute, Option W1 and Option W2, one of which must be selected. The choice depends on whether the UK Housing Grants, Construction and Regeneration Act 1996 as amended by the Local Democracy, Economic Development and Construction Act 2009 ('the Act') applies to the contract. The Act applies to 'construction contracts', which are defined in terms of 'carrying out of construction operations' (Sections 104 and 105 of the Act). This includes such matters as external or internal cleaning of buildings carried out in the course of their repair or restoration. The Act also covers 'painting or decorating the internal or external surfaces of any building or structure'. The Act will not apply to many contracts under the TSC, but will apply to some. Hence it will be necessary to study the Act to decide whether Option W1 or Option W2 should be included.

Option W1 should be selected for contracts to which the Act does not apply, and Option W2 should be selected for contracts to which the Act does apply.

Option X1: Price adjustment for inflation (used only with Options A and C)

Use of this Option has the effect of largely transferring the risk of inflation during the period of the contract to the *Employer*. It uses the formula method. It is appropriate where inflation is high and likely to be variable throughout the period of the contract. Where inflation is low and the service period is, say, one or two years, the risk may not be great. Thus, the Contractor should be able to assess the allowance for inflation in deciding the rates and prices in the Price List. Option X1 is not required under main Option E since the Employer automatically carries the risk of price increases in a cost reimbursable contract.

Option X2: Changes in the law

This Option removes from the Contractor the financial consequences of changes in the law which occur after the Contract Date. This risk may be quite high in some countries or where there is a long service period.

Option X3: Multiple currencies (used only with Option A)

This Option is used when payment to the Contractor is made in more than one currency.

Option X4: Parent company guarantee

Where the Contractor is one of a group of companies, provision of a guarantee of the parent company should provide greater financial security for the Employer.

Option X12: Partnering

This Option can be used for partnering between more than two parties working in a particular area or on a particular asset belonging to the Employer involving a number of different NEC contracts. The parties to NEC contracts which include this Option make up the partnering team. This Option is published also as a separate document for incorporation in NEC contracts which do not have this Option included in their published contracts. The Partnering Option creates a multi-party arrangement rather than a multi-party contract.

The content of the Partnering Option is derived from the *Guide to Project Team Partnering* published by the Construction Industry Council (CIC). Its purpose is to establish the NEC family as an effective contract basis for multi-party partnering. Its incorporation into a TSC enables the service contract to be linked with other NEC contracts such as the Professional Services Contract, the Engineering and Construction Contract and the Engineering and Construction Short Contract. By entering into a contract including Option X12, the parties thereby undertake responsibilities additional to those in the basic NEC contracts. A Core Group manages the conduct of the Partners in accordance with the Partnering Information.

Examples of the use of this Option would be

- maintenance of a public park for a local authority under the TSC,
- extension of the park under the ECC or
- appointment of a landscape architect under the PSC.

Option X13: Performance bond	This Option requires the Contractor to provide a bond to secure his performance of the contract. It therefore provides some protection for the Employer. An Employer may elect not to include it if he has confidence in the Contractor and experience of his previous good performance in the type of work involved in providing the service.
Option X17: Low service damages	This Option is used where the Contractor may not achieve the standards specified in the Service Information. In such cases the specified damages are payable by the Contractor.
Option X18: Limitation of liability	This Option is incorporated in circumstances where acceptance of unlimited liability by a Contractor is not commercially practicable.
Option X19: Task Order	This 'call-off' Option can be used with any of the main Options. With Option A, it determines the amount to be paid to the Contractor for carrying out a specified task. With Option C it determines how the Prices (the target) are decided. With Option E the Price List is used only as a means of forecasting the total of the Prices for the tasks specified in the Task Order.
	Option X19 provides the Employer with the facility to control work on a task-by-task basis. It is intended to be used where it is known that some work of a nature as described in the Service Information, is likely to be required but the precise details and location of which are not known at the Contract Date. When the need arises, the Employer instructs the Contractor to carry out a particular Task in the form of a Task Order. This includes a description of the work to be done, largely compiled from the items on the Price List, and the dates within which it is to be done.
Option X20: Key Performance Indicators (not to be used with Option X12)	Key Performance Indicators (KPIs) are being increasingly used as a means of improving efficiency and encouraging better performance by Contractors with a view to continuous improvement. KPIs are provided for in Option X12 where partnering arrangements are in place. This Option X20 can be used when Option X12 is not used. The procedure in Option X20 requires the establishment of performance targets and regular reporting by the Contractor of his performance measured against the KPIs.
Option Y(UK)2: The Housing Grants, Construction and Regeneration Act 1996	The Option is prepared solely for use on contracts which are subject to the United Kingdom Housing Grants, Construction and Regeneration Act 1996 Part II ('the Act'). The Option should not be used in other circumstances.
	The two principles contained in the Act that affect the NEC Term Service Contract are those related to payment and adjudication. This Option deals only with the payment aspect. The adjudication aspect is dealt with under Option W2. The Parties should consider carefully whether the Act applies to the work in question – see comments under 'The dispute resolution Options'. If the Act does apply, both Options Y(UK)2 and W2 should be included.
Option Y(UK)3: The Contracts (Rights of Third Parties) Act 1999	This Option should only be used within the United Kingdom as it applies only to UK contracts. It has the effect of restricting any rights which third parties may otherwise have by virtue of the provisions of this Act. Only the person(s) and organisation(s) listed in the Contract Data have the right to enforce a term of the contract, and only those terms listed in the Contract Data.
Option Z: Additional conditions of contact	The letter Z is allocated for any additional conditions which the parties may wish to include in the contract. Care should always be exercised in drafting additional clauses to avoid inconsistencies with standard clauses.

CHAPTER 4   PROCEDURE FOR PREPARING A TERM SERVICE CONTRACT

Preparing the tender documents

Where the Employer intends to invite tenders from a number of contractors, the tender documents are prepared by the Employer. These consist of

- Contract Data part one completed in full,
- Service Information,
- Contract Data part two prepared as a pro-forma for completion by each tenderer,
- and Price List (to be priced by tenderer) and
- Form of Tender.

The Employer may also issue Instructions to Tenderers giving such details as the date by which tenders are to be returned, address for return and name of contact for enquiries regarding the tender.

Contract Data part one

This consists of two parts

- statements to be given in all contracts and
- optional statements.

The first entry states the main and secondary Options selected for the contract together with the standard conditions which are incorporated in the contract by reference. It is anticipated that main Option A will be the most frequently used main Option, since in most cases the service to be provided can be clearly defined. Under this Option, the normal payment arrangement will be a monthly fixed amount assuming the service has been provided satisfactorily.

The entry under *service* should be a brief description of the service to be provided. A detailed description is given in the Service Information.

The *Service Manager* is the person appointed by the Employer to carry out the duties and exercise the powers which he has in the contract.

The *Adjudicator* is the person appointed to deal with disputes between the Parties. It is possible that this person can only be named after discussion and negotiation between the parties (see above note under 'Adjudicator'), in which case the entry will remain blank until the appointment has been made.

The entry under 'Affected Property' may refer to a separate document which lists the Employer's property and other property affected or used by the Contractor as stated in the definition.

The entry under 'Service Information' will normally refer to a separate document which specifies in detail the service to be provided by the Contractor. The drafting of the Service Information should be done with great care. Further guidance is given below.

The inclusion of a *period for reply* is designed to promote efficient communication between the various parties. A period of the order of two weeks would normally be specified.

The next entry requires the name of a person or organisation *(Adjudicator nominating body)* which is to nominate a replacement adjudicator if this proves necessary, or to nominate one in the event that one has not already been named in the Contract Data. In the UK construction industry, since the passing of the Housing Grants, Construction and Regeneration Act 1996, a number of adjudicator nominating bodies have been established. Any of these would doubtless be able to appoint a suitable person for service contracts in construction. The *tribunal* would normally be specified as arbitration or litigation in the courts.

The last entry under this section should list the risks which the Employer wishes to be included. The tenderer (or Contractor) adds other risks in part two of the Contract Data.

The first entry under '8 Risks and insurance' states the minimum amount of insurance in respect of loss of or damage to the Employer's property. The second entry states the minimum amount of insurance in respect of things provided by the Employer. The third entry states the minimum amount of insurance in respect of third party claims and the fourth entry states the minimum insurance in relation to the Contractor's employees. The latter may be particularly relevant in those countries which do not have statutory requirements for such insurance.

The meaning of the other entries and those under the optional statements of the Contract Data is self evident when read with the relevant clauses. The entry under the first optional statement would be one of the standard published arbitration procedures. Explanation of the clauses is given in the explanatory notes.

Service Information

Most of the Service Information will be in the form of a specification describing in detail the service which is to be provided by the Contractor. There are several references to the Service Information in the conditions of contract. The Service Information should therefore include the following items as they may apply to a particular contract. The related clause numbers are given in brackets.

Description of the service:

- General description of the service, including drawings where necessary.
- Any constraints on how the Contractor is to provide the service, e.g. restrictions on access, hours of working, sequences of work.

Plant and Materials:

- Materials and workmanship specifications for replacements and renewals to be incorporated as part of the service.
- Requirements for delivery and storage before use in servicing.
- Provision of spares.

Access etc. [15.1 and 15.2]. The right of access to the Affected Property, and other things to be supplied by the Employer.

The Contractor's plan [21.2]. Any information which is required to be shown on the plan, e.g. method of carrying out particular items of work.

Design of Equipment [23.1]. Any design criteria specified by the Employer.

Facilities and other things. Details of others with whom the Contractor will be required to co-operate [25.1]. Any facilities to be provided by the Employer for the use of the Contractor, e.g. power supply, water, welfare, first aid. Similarly any facilities to be provided by the Contractor for the use of the Employer and others whilst carrying out the service [25.2].

Health and safety [27.4]. The particular health and safety requirements such as the safety regulations for the Affected Property. Any health and safety plan as may be required by statute should also be included.

Tests and inspections

40.1. Description of tests and inspections to be carried out by the Contractor, the Service Manager and others.

40.2. Details of which materials, facilities and samples for testing are to be provided by the Contractor and which by the Employer.

41.1. Details of any testing or inspection which is to be carried out before delivery of materials to the Affected Property, together with details of the test or inspection.

Records [52.2 and in Options C and E]. Requirements for records to be kept by the Contractor to enable the Defined Cost to be ascertained and checked.

Equipment [70.2]. List of items of Equipment and other things which the Contractor is to provide for the Employer's use, usually at the end of the service period.

Parent company guarantee [X4.1]. Details of the form of guarantee required by the Employer.

Performance bond [X13.1]. Details of the form of bond required by the Employer. One suggested form of bond is given in Appendix 5. This is based on the standard ICE form of default bond used with the ICE Conditions of Contract.

Task Order programme [X19.6]. Information which should be included on a Task Order programme.

Task Order compensation events [X19.10(4) and (5)]. Things to be provided by the Employer under a Task Order, and the conditions under which the Employer or Others are to work.

Contract Data part two

As for Contract Data part one, entries are in two categories, namely those statements given in all contracts and optional statements.

The *fee percentages* are the figures entered by the tenderer to represent broadly the Contractor's head office overheads and profit in respect of the Contractor's own work and also of subcontract work. They are used to calculate the Fee which is added to Defined Cost. The level of the *fee percentages* is an important factor in assessing the financial aspect of a tender.

The first optional statement applies where tenderers are required to submit with their tenders a plan for carrying out the service. The reference in this entry will be to a separate document which will become the first Contractor's plan of the successful Contractor.

The Price List entry will be a reference to another document (see Appendix 6).

The tendered total of the Prices will be the figure transferred from the total of the Prices column of the Price List.

The Price List

This is the pricing document which is used in a number of different ways according to which main Option applies.

- Option A. The rates and prices in the Price List are used to calculate payments due to the Contractor and to assess compensation events. They are also used for calculating the Prices for a Task Order if Option X19 is included in the contract.
- Option C. The Price List determines the Prices (the target). It may also be used to assess compensation events for the purposes of amending the Prices. It is also used for calculating the Prices for a Task Order if Option X19 is included in the contract.
- Option E. Since this Option creates a cost reimbursable contract, the Price List is relevant only for forecasting and budgeting purposes and for use with Option X19 (if included in the contract). In the case of X19, it is used only to forecast the Prices for the Task Order.

Entries in the first four columns of the Price List (see Appendix 6) are made either by the *Employer* or the tendering contractor. In some cases where the *Employer* enters the items, he may invite tenderers to insert any additional items which they consider necessary. The entries may also be the result of negotiation. There are no standard rules for determining the items to be inserted, but where the tendering contractor prepares the items in the Price List, the *Employer* may choose to specify criteria or guidelines. The last two columns are always completed by the tenderer since these prices comprise a fundamental part of his offer. It is important that the items in the Price List comply with and are consistent with the *Contractor*'s plan.

The items are of two kinds.

- Lump sum items, in which the amount entered in the Price column covers the amount for the work described. Under Option A, this is the amount paid to the *Contractor* when the item of work described has been completed. Under both Options A and C, the lump sums may be used in the pricing of Task Orders where Option X19 is included in the contract. Under Option C, the lump sum prices are relevant in arriving at the Prices (the target). Under Option E the lump sum prices are relevant only in budgeting and in forecasting the Prices of Task Orders under Option X19.
- Quantity-related items, in which the expected quantity is entered in the fourth column and the rate per unit quantity is entered in the fifth column by the tenderer. The quantity is multiplied by the rate to give an amount in the Price column. Under Option A, the *Contractor* is paid for the actual quantity of work done in accordance with the contract. This may be different from the original quantity entered against the item in the Price List as a result of errors in the original quantity, refinement of the calculation of the quantity or other reason. This process is called re-measurement, or sometimes admeasurement. Under Option C, re-measurement of quantity-related items is for the purpose of determining the Prices (the target). The rates entered against quantity-related items may be used in all main Options in relation to assessing compensation events and in pricing of Task Orders under Option X19 in a similar way to lump sum items.

Pricing of the Price List should cover all the work required to comply with the Service Information. In the case of Option A, for example, the total of the Prices is the payment to be made to the Contractor for the work done by the Contractor in providing the service described in the Service Information, but subject to re-measurement.

Where the Contractor is paid after different periods of time, say at the end of each calendar month, the total number of months is entered in the Expected Quantity column. The amount per month for carrying out the work described in the Description column is entered in the Rate column. The total amount to be paid to the Contractor for providing the service described throughout the service period is calculated from the number of time periods multiplied by the rate per period.

Inviting tenders

It is common practice to issue instructions to tenderers. These instructions do not become part of the contract documents as they are intended merely to give guidance to those tendering. For example, the Employer may wish tendering contractors to submit information about how they are proposing to provide the service. If so, the Contractor's plan submitted with the tender is included in part two of the Contract Data. When a tender is accepted, the plan becomes the first Accepted Plan.

The instructions to tenderers should also state which management functions are to be performed by the people to be identified in the Contract Data.

A complete form of tender should be submitted, comprising the Contractor's formal offer to Provide the Service. A sample form for this purpose is given in Appendix 2.

Preparing a tender

Preparing a tender will consist of completing the entries in part two of the Contract Data and completing and pricing the Price List. For both of these a thorough understanding of the conditions of contract is essential The tenderer should also be clear on the nature of the service to be provided by the Contractor as detailed in the Service Information and other contract documents.

Assessing tenders

To ensure equal treatment of all tenderers and to assist in their understanding of the Employer's requirements, the criteria upon which tenders are to be assessed and the weight given to various factors should be clearly stated in the instructions to tenderers. These criteria may include such matters as management of the Contractor's organisation, past record of experience of similar work, health and safety record as well as the financial aspect. It is important that all documents submitted with tenders are carefully examined, as once accepted a tender becomes contractually binding on both Parties. This particularly applies to the Contractor's plan if submitted as part of the tender. A number of compensation events refer to dates on the Contractor's plan. Thus careful examination by the Employer of these dates and their effects is essential.

Creating the contract

Frequently, negotiations with one or more tenderers are necessary to clarify intentions, to agree amendments, to eliminate qualifications which are not acceptable to the Employer and to discuss the Contractor's plan. It is important to minimise these negotiations since extended discussions can result in abuse of the tendering process. This can be achieved by careful preparation of tender documents and instructions to tenderers and by stating award criteria in objective terms.

The creation of a contract can be by means of acceptance of a tender or a revised tender or by means of acceptance by the Contractor of a counter-offer prepared by or on behalf of the Employer. A binding contract is thus created, although some Employers may require such acceptance being subject to a formal agreement. A suitable form of agreement is included in Appendix 3, but Employers often have their own standard forms. Essentially, they record the agreement between the two Parties and identify the documents which make up the contract.

CHAPTER 5   EXPLANATORY NOTES ON THE CLAUSES OF THE TERM SERVICE CONTRACT

1 General

CORE CLAUSES

Actions **10**

10.1 This clause obliges the *Employer*, the *Contractor* and the *Service Manager* to do everything which the contract states they are to do. It is the only clause which uses the future tense. For simplicity, everything else is in the present tense. Where actions are permitted but not obligatory, the term 'may' is used.

The other statement specifies *how* the parties are to act. This is a fundamental requirement of all contracts in the NEC family of contracts and is designed to encourage a collaborative rather than a confrontational approach to management of the contract.

Identified and defined terms **11**

11.1 The main definitions used in the contract are given in clause 11. Other definitions are given in optional clauses where they are specific to a particular Option. The conventions for italics and capital initials as used in the TSC are used also in this section of the guidance notes.

11.2 (1) The definition of the Accepted Plan allows for the two situations where there may or may not have been a requirement for tenderers to submit a plan with their tenders. A tender plan is identified in part two of the Contract Data and becomes the Accepted Plan when the contract comes into existence. If a tender plan is intended to become the Accepted Plan, it should conform to the requirements of clause 21.

(2) The definition of Affected Property is intended to cover any property which may be affected by the *Contractor*'s activities in Providing the Service during the *service period.* It is however restricted to property described in the Contract Data and in many contracts would consist mostly of the *Employer*'s property. Its main relevance is in relation to early warning (clause 16) and compensation events. Under the latter, a change to Affected Property which affects the *Contractor*'s cost of Providing the Service may constitute a compensation event.

(3) The Contract Date is used to define the date when the contract comes into existence, regardless of the means by which this is achieved.

(4) Any departure from the *service* as specified in the contract constitutes a Defect.

(5) This definition of Defined Cost applies to all main Options and includes four basic elements. The *Employer* is protected against artificially inflated prices for any of these elements by clause 52.1. This requires any amounts included in Defined Cost to be at prices which are at open market or competitively tendered levels.

(6) Disallowed Cost is deducted In the assessment of Defined Cost. There are two deductions concerning insurances.

The first, in the penultimate bullet, avoids the *Employer* having to pay for costs which the *Contractor* is required by the contract to insure against, for example the theft of Equipment. In that case the full cost of the event is deducted, regardless of what the *Contractor* can recover from his insurers. Therefore in this respect the *Contractor* is at risk for any insurance excesses he has, or if he fails to take out the insurances the contract requires.

The second, which is the final deduction listed in clause 11.2(6), ensures that the *Contractor* does not receive double payment as a result of payment of any other insurance he has voluntarily taken out Here the deduction is limited to the amount the *Contractor* has actually received from his insurers.

(7) The definition of Equipment covers such things as *Contractor*'s plant, vehicles, consumables, tools, temporary works, cabins and other site facilities. Some equipment may be provided by the *Employer* for the *Contractor*'s use during the *service period* (clause 70.1) at the end of which it is returned to the *Employer*, but this falls outside this definition. If the Service Information so requires, Equipment provided by the *Contractor* may be transferred to the *Employer* for his further use at the end of the *service period* (clause 70.2).

(8) Any costs of the *Contractor* not included in Defined Cost are deemed to be included, together with profit, in the Fee (clause 52.1). It is calculated from the relevant *fee percentage* stated in part two of the Contract Data. It may be used for assessing compensation events under all main Options, and in calculating payments to the *Contractor* (Price for Services Provided to Date – PSPD) under Options C and E.

(9) The term 'Others' provides a convenient means of reference to people and organisations not directly involved in the contract.

(11) Items temporarily used in Providing the Service but which are removed at or before the end of the *service period* are excluded from Plant and Materials.

(14) The Risk Register provides a means of identifying and managing risk at the beginning of and throughout the *service period*. The number and type of risks will vary and will depend on many factors, such as nature of the *service*, location and type of Affected Property and changes in the Service Information. The risks listed in both parts of the Contract Data are those identified at the Contract Date. Other risks will be added to the Risk Register as a result of the early warning procedures (clause 16). Allocation of risk between *Employer* and *Contractor* is dealt with in the contract. The main purpose of the early warning procedure is to identify further risks as soon as possible, eliminate them where possible or reduce them and motivate the Parties to co-operate in mitigating their effect.

(15) Service Information is information about the *service* to be provided. Service Information can be varied by the *Service Manager* during the course of the contract (clause 14.3).

In certain cases, additional Service Information may be provided by the *Contractor*. This information relates to the *Contractor*'s plan and is included in Contract Data part two.

(16) The definition of Subcontractor excludes a supplier to the *Contractor* except as stated in this clause.

Communications 13

13.1   The phrase 'in a form which can be read, copied and recorded' includes a document sent by post, cable, electronic mail, facsimile transmission, and on disc, magnetic tape or other electronic means.

13.3   This clause together with clause 13.4 establishes the use of a *period for reply* wherever the term (identified in the Contract Data part one) is used in the *conditions of contract*. In some circumstances it may be appropriate to specify more than one *period for reply* in the Contract Data.

13.5   This clause provides for extending the *period for reply* by agreement.

13.6   The *Service Manager* issues payment certificates under clause 51.1. He may also issue a termination certificate under clause 90.1, and a final payment certificate after termination under clause 90.4.

13.7   The requirement to notify information separately is intended to avoid important things being overlooked. For example, submission of a revised plan showing a change of method does not count as an early warning of a matter which could impair an activity. Requiring separate notices also makes it easier to track the procedure following the issue of a notice.

13.8   The TSC contains a number of examples of situations in which a *Service Manager* must either accept or reject a document which contains proposals submitted by the *Contractor*. In each such case, grounds for rejecting the submission are stated. This does not prevent the *Service Manager* from rejecting the submission for other reasons, but if he does so, the rejection is a compensation event (clause 60.1(8)). This arrangement limits the *Contractor*'s risk and provides more objective criteria on which to judge acceptance.

The *Service Manager*   14

14.1   The *Service Manager* is the key person involved in the management of the contract from the *Employer*'s point of view. His duties and authority are described in the clauses of the contract. They are not summarised in a single clause. It is assumed that the *Service Manager* will confer with the *Employer* as necessary, in deciding which of various actions to take and in making other decisions which affect the outcome of the contract. For the purposes of the contract almost all dealings with the *Contractor* are handled by the *Service Manager*. If the *Service Manager* needs to consult the *Employer,* the internal arrangements between them should be such that the contractual time limits can be achieved.

14.2   On major service contracts requiring much supervision, it is normal for the *Service Manager* to have staff to help him to carry out his duties. This clause enables him to delegate specific duties and authorities under the contract to particular people. Delegation of particular duties or authorities does not prevent the *Service Manager* from also acting himself.

14.3   This clause gives the *Service Manager* a wide power. An instruction under this clause may be an addition to or deletion of part of the Service Information as well as alterations to it. All such changes are potentially compensation events as set out in clause 60.1(1).

***Employer* provides right of   15
access and things   15.1**   The *Employer* is required to provide the legal right of access to Affected Property. He may not be required to provide the physical access occupied by Others. However, anything he is to provide is to be stated in the Service Information and failure to provide it constitutes a compensation event (clause 60.1(3)).

Early warning   16

16.1   The purpose of this very important clause is to make binding the obligation to warn as soon as possible of anything which may affect the cost and the proper performance of the *service* in relation to timing and effectiveness. The sanction for failure by the *Contractor* to give early warning is to reduce payment due to him for a related compensation event (clause 63.6).

16.2   This clause authorises the *Service Manager* or *Contractor* to call a risk reduction meeting at any time to discuss problems or potential problems of which notice has been given so that they can be considered and dealt with in good time. Such problems may include, for example, effects of bad weather, failure of a Subcontractor or supplier to perform and interference by a third party with an access. It may be agreed that other people, who may be able to assist in solving the problem, should attend the meeting.

16.3   This clause provides the items for the agenda of the risk reduction meeting. The parties attending are required to co-operate in solving the problem irrespective of where the financial liability may rest. The procedure set out in the clause gives priority to dealing with the problem rather than to contractual liability.

16.4   The decisions made at a risk reduction meeting are recorded on the Risk Register.

Ambiguities and inconsistencies   **17**

17.1   This clause is intended to ensure that action is taken as soon as possible to deal with ambiguities and inconsistencies noticed in the contract documents. There is no stated precedence of documents. The *Service Manager* has the responsibility of resolving the ambiguity or inconsistency in the documents. An instruction to change the Service Information to resolve an ambiguity or inconsistency is a compensation event provided it is covered by clause 60.1(1).

Illegal and impossible requirements   **18**

18.1   Any instruction changing the Service Information in order to resolve a requirement in the Service Information which is illegal or impossible is a compensation event (clause 60.1(1)).

MAIN OPTION CLAUSES

Option A: Priced contract with price list

Identified and defined terms   **11**

11.2   (17) The Price for Services Provided to Date (PSPD) is the Price List Prices for those lump sum items of work which have been completed, and, for quantity-related items, the quantity completed by the *Contractor* multiplied by the rate.

(19) The Prices are the basis on which the PSPD is calculated.

Option C: Target contract with price list

Identified and defined terms   **11**

11.2   (18) As Option C is a form of cost reimbursable contract, the PSPD is based on Defined Cost as defined in core clause 11.2(5). It consists of amounts calculated from amounts which the *Contractor* has paid.

(20) The Prices in this Option are not used to determine the PSPD. They are used instead to calculate the target whenever the *Contractor*'s share needs to be calculated (see clause 54).

Option E: Cost reimbursable contract

Identified and defined terms   **11**

11.2   (18) This definition is identical to that of the PSPD in Option C.

(21) In this Option, the Prices are used only for forecasting purposes (clause 20.4).

2 The *Contractor*'s main responsibilities

CORE CLAUSES

This section sets out the *Contractor*'s main responsibilities. Other sections deal with particular responsibilities appropriate to the section heading.

Providing the Service 20

20.1   This clause states the *Contractor*'s basic obligation. 'Provide the Service' is defined in clause 11.2(12). It includes supplying all the necessary resources to achieve the end result. The Service Information provided by the *Employer* should state everything which is intended concerning the *service* which the *Contractor* is to provide.

20.2   This clause places some restraint on how the *Contractor* is to Provide the Service. It is also intended to permit normal everyday use of Affected Property to continue, as far as practicable consistent with the work being done by the *Contractor*. The *Contractor*'s obligation is therefore stated in general terms. In most service contracts, the *Contractor*'s activities will interfere with the *Employer*'s normal 'enjoyment' of the Affected Property.

The *Contractor*'s plan 21

21.1   Provision is made in the Contract Data for a *Contractor*'s plan to be identified in the Contract Data part two or to be submitted by the *Contractor* within a period stated in the Contract Data part one.

The plan is an important document for administering the contract. It informs the *Employer* and the *Service Manager* of the *Contractor*'s detailed intentions of how he is to Provide the Service. It enables the *Service Manager* to monitor the *Contractor*'s performance and to assess the effects of compensation events.

Employers will normally elect to have the plan submitted with tenders in order to judge whether a tenderer has fully understood his obligations and whether he is able to do the work in the time periods proposed using the methods and resources proposed. Any doubts on these matters can then be discussed and resolved after submission of tenders. In accepting a tender which includes a *Contractor*'s plan, it is important that the *Employer* makes clear that such acceptance does not warrant that the methods and resources are adequate. Acceptance of a plan is not a condition precedent to the *Contractor* proceeding with his work. Failure to accept a plan or revised plan does not require the *Contractor* to stop work.

Such is the importance of the plan that where the *Contractor* is required to submit a first plan after the Contract Date, a sanction is included if the *Contractor* fails to do so (clause 50.3).

When the whole of the *services* are being instructed under Task Orders using Option X19 the plan will, in effect, contain little more than the basic contract information. It would include any specific information required by the Service Information; for example the arrangements for consulting over a Task Order or for mobilising following the issue of a Task Order.

21.2   This clause lists the information which the *Contractor* is required to show on each plan submitted for acceptance. Statements of how the *Contractor* plans to do his work are important items on the list. They consist of descriptions of working methods as well as details of the resources, including Equipment, the *Contractor* intends to use. Thus any reference in the contract to the plan includes these statements. This means for example that a *Contractor*'s quotation submitted in relation to a compensation event which includes alterations to the plan may also include revised working methods and resources (clause 62.2).

The *Contractor*'s time risk allowances are to be shown on the plan as allowances attached to the duration of each activity. These are periods of time which the *Contractor* allows for matters which are at his risk.

The provision for health and safety matters should allow for any statutory procedures, as well as those specifically mentioned in the Service Information.

Three compensation events – clauses 60.1(2), (3) and (5) – refer to dates or times in the Accepted Plan and failure to adhere to these may result in additional compensation to the *Contractor*. Thus it is important when the *Service Manager* is scrutinising the plan prior to acceptance that he considers carefully these particular dates and times.

21.3 This clause lists reasons why a *Service Manager* may decide not to accept a plan or revised plan. Rejection by the *Service Manager* of a plan for reasons other than those noted is a compensation event (clause 60.1(8)). The *Service Manager* is required to respond within two weeks, and if the reply is non-acceptance, the *Contractor* is required to re-submit within the *period for reply*.

Revising the Contractor's plan 22

22.1 This clause states the two basic matters which are to be shown on a revised plan. If a compensation event affects the *Contractor*'s plan, alterations to the existing plan are to be included as part of the *Contractor*'s quotation (clause 62.2).

The *Service Manager* should note, in reviewing a submitted revised plan, any changes to the dates by which the *Employer* is required to provide access, acceptances, information, etc. He should be prepared to accept a plan with earlier dates if this is acceptable to the *Employer*. After acceptance, subsequent failure by the *Employer* to meet these earlier dates is a compensation event.

Failure by the *Contractor* to submit a revised plan is of considerable disadvantage to the *Contractor* in that if a compensation event occurs, the *Service Manager* may assess it entirely on the basis of his own judgement (clause 64.1). Thus it is in the *Contractor*'s interests to keep the plan up to date.

Design of Equipment 23

23.1 This clause allows the *Service Manager* to accept the *Contractor*'s design of Equipment without affecting the *Contractor*'s responsibilities (clause 14.1). The *Contractor* is still liable if, after having made the Equipment to details which have been accepted, it fails because it did not comply with the Service Information. The clause gives three criteria for design of the Equipment. Failure to comply gives the *Service Manager* the right, but not the obligation, to reject the design.

There is no constraint on the *Contractor* proceeding even if the design of an item of Equipment has not been accepted. The *Service Manager* should seek details of Equipment well in advance of when the work is going to be done (prompted by what he sees on the *Contractor*'s plan) so that he can register any dissatisfaction with the proposals in good time.

People 24

24.1 This clause gives reasons for not accepting a proposed replacement for a key person. It does not preclude the *Service Manager* from accepting a person with qualifications or experience which are inferior to those of the listed person if he is satisfied that such a person will be suitable for the position.

24.2 This clause provides the authority for the *Service Manager*, on behalf of the *Employer*, to have a *Contractor*'s employee removed from work on the contract. Possible reasons for exercising this authority may include:

- security
- health and safety (including communicable disease)
- disorderly behaviour prejudicing the *Employer*'s operations.

Working with the *Employer* and Others **25**

25.1   The *Contractor*'s duty to co-operate with Others is expressed in general terms only – the detailed requirements will depend on the particular circumstances of the *service* being provided and the Affected Property. Where the *Contractor*'s work may affect or interfere with the activities of the *Employer* or Others, it is important that interfaces in respect of physical location and timing are agreed by all parties and shown on the *Contractor*'s plan. The exchange of information on health and safety matters is particularly important in order to comply with the law as well as with the contract.

25.2   This clause states the obligations of the Parties to provide facilities and other things. Details of all such requirements should be included in the Service Information. Failure to fulfil these obligations may result in a compensation event (if the *Employer* defaults – clause 60.1(3)) or payment to the *Employer* by the *Contractor* (if the *Contractor* defaults).

Subcontracting **26**

26.2   This clause provides that the *Contractor* may subcontract parts of his work provided the *Service Manager* accepts the proposed Subcontractors. Where national or international law requires, the Service Information should state the award criteria for subcontracts. Acceptance of a Subcontractor cannot be withdrawn later, provided his appointment complies with these clauses.

Other responsibilities **27**

27.1   This clause requires the *Contractor* to obtain the requisite approvals of his plan from planning authorities, nuclear inspectorates or others who may have the duty or authority to approve his proposals.

27.2   It is important that the *Service Manager* has the right to visit places where work is being carried out in connection with the contract. This includes right of access to suppliers' and Subcontractors' premises to allow inspection and testing, and to check progress.

27.3   Various clauses in the contract give the *Service Manager* authority to issue instructions to the *Contractor*. These instructions should be given within the limits and for the reasons expressly stated. If for any reason the *Contractor* disagrees with an instruction, having exhausted the procedures in the contract for dealing with such a situation, his remedy is follow the disputes procedure in Option W1 or W2 as appropriate. He should not to refuse to obey the instruction.

27.4   Any specific health and safety requirements relating to the Affected Property and the activities of the *Contractor* in providing the *service* should be stated in the Service Information. These are additional to any obligations the *Contractor* may have under national law.

MAIN OPTION CLAUSES

Option A: Priced contract with price list

Providing the Service **20**

20.5   An important aspect of the management of any contract is to monitor the forecast final out-turn cost. This is more straightforward in the case of Option A, than Options C and E.

Option C: Target contract with price list

Providing the Service **20**

20.4   An important aspect of the management of a cost reimbursement contract is to monitor the forecast final out-turn cost. This clause requires the *Contractor* to consult with the *Service Manager* for this purpose taking account of such matters as compensation events and changes in quantities of work.

Subcontracting **26**

26.4 The terms of a subcontract assume greater importance for the *Employer* in the case of a cost reimbursable contract (Options C and E) than for a Priced contract (Option A) – hence this additional clause.

Option E: Cost reimbursable contract

Providing the Service **20**

20.4 An important aspect of the management of a cost reimbursement contract is to monitor the forecast final out-turn cost. This clause requires the *Contractor* to consult with the *Service Manager* for this purpose taking account of such matters as compensation events and changes in quantities of work.

Subcontracting **26**

26.4 The terms of a subcontract assume greater importance for the *Employer* in the case of a cost reimbursable contract (Options C and E) than for a Priced contract (Option A) – hence this additional clause.

3 Time

CORE CLAUSES

Starting and the service period **30**

30.1 The *starting date* and the *service period* are stated in the Contract Data. If the procurement process and appointment of the *Contractor* takes longer than anticipated, it may be necessary to adjust the *starting date* by agreement before the Contract Date. The *Employer* is required to give the *Contractor* access as shown on the Accepted Plan to enable the *Contractor* to start work (clause 31.1).

Access **31**

31.1 Any constraints on the *Contractor*'s access to Affected Property should be stated in the Service Information so that the *Contractor* can prepare his plan accordingly. Once the *Service Manager* has accepted the plan, the dates of access are binding on the *Employer*. Failure to provide such access constitutes a compensation event.

Where the *service* requires the *Contractor* to gain access to, say, a large number of residential properties, the actual access may have to be provided by the occupiers. It may not be possible or practicable to include each separate access, including dates, etc, on the *Contractor*'s plan. It is possible that on a particular day, the occupier is not able to grant the *Contractor* access. Full details of the procedures to be followed in such cases should be included in the Service Information.

Instructions to stop or not to start work **32**

32.1 This clause gives the *Service Manager* authority to control the stopping and re-starting of work for any reason, for example where there is risk of injury to people or damage to property. An instruction given under this clause constitutes a compensation event, but if it arises from a fault of the *Contractor*, the Prices are not changed (clause 61.4). In certain circumstances, if the *Service Manager* fails to instruct the re-start of work within thirteen weeks of instructing work to stop, either Party may be entitled to terminate the contract (clause 91.6).

4 Testing and Defects

CORE CLAUSES

The *Contractor*'s responsibility for quality is part of his duty to Provide the Service (clause 20.1) as defined in clause 11.2(13). The quality standards to be achieved by the *Contractor* should be specified in the Service Information. These standards provide the basis on which the existence of Defects is judged. The *Service Manager* may act on the *Employer*'s behalf to check the *Contractor*'s attainment of the specified standards.

The *Employer* may, as an alternative to specifying quality standards, require the *Contractor* to provide proposals for his quality plan with his tender, and incorporate them in the Service Information.

Tests and inspections 40

40.1 Clause 40 does not apply to tests and inspections done by the *Contractor* for his own purposes.

40.2 Tests should be specified in the Service Information with respect to

- nature of the tests,
- when they are to be done,
- where they are to be done,
- who does the test,
- who provides materials, facilities and samples and
- objectives and procedures.

Additional tests may be instructed by the *Service Manager* by changing the Service Information. Such an instruction constitutes a compensation event (clause 60.1(1)).

40.3 This clause deals with four matters

- procedure for notifying when testing is to be done,
- requirement to notify test results,
- timing of notifying the *Service Manager* of testing or inspection and
- right of the *Service Manager* to observe the *Contractor*'s tests.

The *Contractor* and *Service Manager* are each required to give the other advance notice of tests and inspections which each is to carry out. This enables both parties to be fully informed and to take any action they wish to take, e.g. early discussion of the consequences of a test which fails.

40.4 The *Contractor* has a general obligation to correct Defects. In some cases, such as where the *Contractor* is required to do work at a specific time and he does not do so, remedying of the Defect becomes impossible. The sanction then is a financial one, namely payment to the *Employer* under clause 42.1.

40.5 Unnecessary delay by the *Service Manager* in doing a test or inspection constitutes a compensation event – clause 60.1(9). Some payments to the *Contractor* may be conditional upon doing particular tests to show that the work has been done satisfactorily. In the case of some tests and inspection, it may be possible to specify timing in the Service Information. This avoids the subjective judgement on what constitutes unnecessary delay.

40.6 This clause protects the *Employer* against possible extra costs caused by the *Contractor* doing defective work.

Testing and inspection before delivery	**41**
	41.1

The purpose of this clause is to avoid expense in having to transport Plant and Materials back to the place of manufacture if testing and inspection reveal Defects.

Notifying and correcting Defects	**42**
	42.1

The intention of this clause is to enable Defects to be identified as soon as possible so that they can be dealt with promptly. However the *Contractor*'s obligation is to correct a Defect as soon as he knows about it, and not wait for the *Service Manager* to act.

42.2 The Service Information may include a requirement for satisfactory completion of certain tests and acceptance by the *Service Manager* of standards which will enable the *Employer* to resume use of the asset. There is no fixed time within which the *Contractor* is required to correct a Defect or make good an omission as this will depend on the circumstances of each particular case. The test to be applied in each such case is 'At what time will the Defect or omission and its correction or making good cause the minimum adverse effect on the *Employer* or Others?'

42.3 The procedure in this clause allows the *Contractor* access to correct a Defect, at a time which will be at the *Employer*'s convenience.

Accepting Defects	**43**
	43.1

Although a Defect may be minor, its correction may be costly to the *Contractor* and may delay completion by a considerable time. Its correction may also cause inconvenience to the *Employer* out of all proportion to the benefits gained. Correction of the Defect may even have become impossible because of the passage of time. This clause gives a procedure within the contract for accepting a Defect in these circumstances. Either the *Contractor* or the *Service Manager* may propose a change to the Service Information solely to avoid the need to correct a Defect. The other is not obliged to accept the proposal.

The *Contractor*'s quotation for the proposed change will show a reduction in the Prices. In some cases the reduction may be nominal. For example, a nominal price reduction may be acceptable if the effect of the change to the Service Information is not detrimental and if the alternative of correcting the Defect will be of inconvenience to the *Employer*.

If the quotation is not acceptable, no further action is necessary. If the quotation is accepted by the *Service Manager*, the Service Information and the Prices change accordingly. Such a change to the Service Information is not a compensation event (clause 60.1(1)).

5 Payment

CORE CLAUSES

Assessing the amount due **50**

50.1 This clause defines 'assessment dates' from which the dates of both certification and payment are calculated. The first assessment date is determined by the *Service Manager*, preferably after discussion with the *Contractor*, with a view to satisfying the internal procedures of both the *Employer* and the *Contractor*. Thereafter, assessment dates occur after each *assessment interval* until four weeks after the end of the *service period*.

50.2 The basic amount due to the *Contractor* is the Price for Services Provided to Date (PSPD). All other payments such as VAT and sales tax, and payments by the *Contractor* for failure to correct Defects, are added to or deducted from the PSPD to calculate the amount due. The content of the PSPD varies according to which main Option is used.

Under the United Kingdom's VAT regulations, payment of VAT by the *Employer* to the *Contractor* is made in response to a VAT invoice provided by the *Contractor*. The *Service Manager* and the *Contractor* should therefore make arrangements to ensure that

- the correct levels of VAT are included in the amount due and
- the *Contractor*'s VAT invoice is provided for attachment to the *Service Manager*'s certificate.

If the *Employer* uses a self billing system, a *Contractor*'s invoice is not needed and the *Employer*'s remittance document becomes the VAT invoice.

50.3 This clause provides a strong motivation for the *Contractor* to submit a plan which contains the information required by the contract. If a plan is required to be submitted with the tender, the plan is identified in the Contract Data at the Contract Date. In this situation, an Accepted Plan already exists and no amount can be retained.

If a plan is not identified in the Contract Data, it is vitally important for the management of the contract that a plan complying with clause 21 is submitted within the period stated in the Contract Data. If the *Contractor* has not submitted a plan within this time, an amount can be retained from the amount due, as stated in this clause, until the *Contractor* has submitted a plan.

50.4 Although assessments of the amount due are the responsibility of the *Service Manager* (clause 50.1), he takes account of any submissions by the *Contractor* and provides details of his assessment.

Payment **51**

51.1 The latest dates by which the *Service Manager* certifies payments are fixed throughout a contract as each is related to an assessment date. In the majority of cases, certification will be of payment to the *Contractor*.

51.2 The latest dates by which payments are due to be made are also fixed throughout a contract as each is related to an assessment date. Interest is due to the receiving party, either *Employer* or *Contractor*, if a payment is not made within the stated period after the assessment date. The *Service Manager* should

- certify payment as early as possible within the week after the assessment date and
- before the Contract Date, check that the *Employer* is able to pay within the stated period after the assessment date.

The principle that interest is due from the latest date that payment should have been made is applied throughout the contract.

51.3 The same principles on interest due apply to later corrections to certified amounts (including any due to compensation events) made by the *Service Manager* or decided by the *Adjudicator* or the *tribunal*. The last sentence of this clause refers to interest being calculated from the date upon which the increased amount would have been certified if there had been no dispute or mistake.

51.4 The *interest rate* stated in part one of the Contract Data should be a reliable annual base rate applicable to the territory in which the work is to be done plus a percentage to represent the current commercial rates. This may be, for example, 2% above the base rate. Simple interest at the *interest rate* applies for periods less than one year.

Defined Cost 52

52.1 Defined Cost is defined in clause 11.2(5) and is the same for all main Options. The first sentence of this clause seeks to define the boundary between the *Contractor*'s head office overheads and other costs. But the *fee percentages* will include profit and any other costs not covered by Defined Cost.

MAIN OPTION CLAUSES

Option A: Priced contract with price list

The Price List 54

54.1 This clause emphasises the fact that the Price List is only a payment document. It cannot be used to determine what the *Contractor* is to do or what service he is to provide. It is used for different purposes according to which main Option applies.

- Option A – used to determine the Prices and the PSPD.
- Option C – used to determine only the Prices and sometimes to assess compensation events. This in turn is used to calculate the *Contractor*'s share under clause 53.
- Option E – used only for forecasting cost.

54.2 The *Contractor* is free to change the *Contractor*'s plan as he wishes but the Accepted Plan and the Price List must always be compatible. A Price List which contains items that do not represent the *Contractor*'s proposed activities and methods of working will create difficulties in determining payments due. Hence, it is important that the Price List relates directly to the Accepted Plan and is compatible with it.

54.3 This clause states the criteria by which changes to the Price List are to be judged. For instance, any change to the Prices should not upset the balance of pricing which existed in the original Price List. The total of the Prices must not be changed except as a result of a compensation event or correction of quantities. The criteria do not attempt to restrict changes to cash flow resulting from revisions to the Price List.

Option C: Target contract with price list

Assessing the amount due 50

50.6 As the *Contractor* is paid Defined Cost, he is reimbursed by the *Employer* in the same currency as the payments made by him. Nevertheless, the Fee and the *Contractor*'s share are paid in the *currency of this contract*. Calculations are based on the *exchange rates*.

Defined Cost **52**

52.2   This clause lists the accounts and records which the *Contractor* is required to keep and which are essential for calculating Defined Cost. Details of any specific records required should be given in the Service Information.

The *Contractor*'s share **53**

53.1   This clause states how the *Contractor*'s share is calculated. The *share ranges* are decided by the *Employer* and stated in part one of the Contract Data.

53.2   This clause states the main principle of target contracts whereby the *Contractor* receives a share of any savings and pays a share of any excess when the PSPD is compared to the target (the total of the Prices) at specified times.

For example, assume that the Contract Data states that

- The *Contractor*'s *share percentages* and the *share ranges* are

Share range	Contractor's share percentage
less than 80%	15%
from 80% to 90%	30%
from 90% to 110%	50%
greater than 110%	20%

If on the first date stated in the Contract Data for assessing the *Contractor*'s share the total of the Prices (having been adjusted for compensation events and re-measurement of quantities) is £100,000, the Contract Data becomes in effect

PSPD	Contractor's share percentage
less than £80,000	15%
from £80,000 to £90,000	30%
from £90,000 to £110,000	50%
greater than £110,000	20%

An example of the possible outcome is

PSPD = £75,000

Saving under total of the Prices = £25,000, comprising three increments

less than £80,000 = £5,000 @ 15%	= £750
£80,000 to £90,000 = £10,000 @ 30%	= £3,000
£90,000 to £110,000 = £10,000 @ 50%	= £5,000
Contractor's share	= £8,750
(paid by *Employer*)	

The other potential source of profit for the *Contractor* is the Fee. The *Contractor*'s *share percentages* should be determined in a particular contract to provide the appropriate level of incentive to the *Contractor* to minimise the PSPD. The extent of financial risk to the Parties in the event of the final PSPD exceeding the total of the Prices can be varied between two extremes

- a guaranteed maximum price to the *Employer* can be achieved by stating the *Contractor*'s *share percentage* to be 100% above that price and
- a maximum payment to the *Contractor* can be achieved by stating the *Contractor*'s *share percentage* to be 0% above a stated price.

53.3   Payment of the target share is made at intervals – at the dates stated in the Contract Data. These intervals may be say six or twelve months throughout the *service period*.

The Price List **54**

54.1   This clause emphasises the fact that the Price List is only a payment document. It cannot be used to determine what the *Contractor* is to do or what service he is to provide. It is used for different purposes according to which main Option applies.

- Option A – used to determine the Prices and the PSPD.
- Option C – used to determine only the Prices and sometimes to assess compensation events. This in turn is used to calculate the *Contractor*'s share under clause 53.
- Option E – used only for forecasting cost.

54.2   The *Contractor* is free to change the *Contractor*'s plan as he wishes but the Accepted Plan and the Price List must always be compatible. A Price List which contains items that do not represent the *Contractor*'s proposed activities and methods of working will create difficulties in determining payments due. Hence, it is important that the Price List relates directly to the Accepted Plan and is compatible with it.

54.3   This clause states the criteria by which changes to the Price List are to be judged. For instance, any change to the Prices should not upset the balance of pricing which existed in the original Price List. The total of the Prices must not be changed except as a result of a compensation event or the correction of quantities. The criteria do not attempt to restrict changes to cash flow resulting from revisions to the Price List.

Option E: Cost reimbursable contract

Assessing the amount due **50**

50.7   As the *Contractor* is paid Defined Cost, he is reimbursed by the *Employer* in the same currency as the payments made by him. Nevertheless, the Fee is paid in the *currency of this contract*. Calculations are based on the *exchange rates*.

Defined Cost **52**

52.2   This clause lists the accounts and records which the *Contractor* is required to keep and which are essential for calculating Defined Cost. Details of any specific records required should be given in the Service Information.

6 Compensation events

CORE CLAUSES

Compensation events 60	Compensation events are events which, if they occur and do not arise from the *Contractor*'s fault, entitle the *Contractor* to be compensated for any effect the event may have on the Prices. A compensation event will normally result in additional payment to the *Contractor* but in a few cases may result in reduced payment.

Compensation events are listed in the core clauses. Further compensation events are stated in Options X2, X12 and X19 (the latter lists a further seven compensation events). The main list is in clause 60.1; this includes events (1) to (14).

Option Z may be used by the *Employer* to insert additional compensation events. The effect of such additions is to transfer the financial risk of the events from the *Contractor* to the *Employer*. The event must be described precisely.

Changing the Service 60.1 Information (1)	Changes to the *service* are made by a *Service Manager*'s instruction to change the Service Information. The authority given to the *Service Manager* for this purpose is in clause 14.3. Changes may comprise deletions from, or additions to, the Service Information. There may be many reasons for changing the Service Information, e.g. a change made to eliminate an illegality or impossibility (clause 18) or to resolve an ambiguity or inconsistency (clause 17).

The clause states two exceptions to a change to the Service Information being a compensation event.

- The procedure for accepting a Defect is stated in clause 43. An instruction to change the Service Information after acceptance of the *Contractor*'s quotation under clause 43.1 is not a compensation event.
- A change to the *Contractor*'s plan made at his own request is not a compensation event. The clause also gives precedence to the Service Information in part one of the Contract Data over the Service Information in part two of the Contract Data. Thus the *Contractor* should ensure that the Service Information he prepares and submits with his tender as part two of the Contract Data complies with the requirements of the Service Information in part one of the Contract Data. (See also notes on clause 21.2.)

Access (2)	The *Employer*'s obligation to provide the right of access is stated in clause 31.1.
Provision by the *Employer* (3)	The Service Information should give details of anything which the *Employer* is to provide, such as equipment, Plant and Materials, and of any restrictions on when it is to be provided. The *Contractor* is required to include this information in his plan under clause 21.2.
Stopping work (4)	Clause 32.1 gives the *Service Manager* authority to instruct the *Contractor* to stop or not to start work. There are several reasons why the *Service Manager* may wish to give such an instruction, e.g. for reasons of safety.
Work of the *Employer* or (5) Others	The Service Information should give details of the order and timing of work to be done by the *Employer* and Others. The *Contractor* is required to include this in the information on his plan under clause 21.2.

Reply to a communication	(6)	Various periods are given in particular clauses for reply by the *Service Manager* and a general *period for reply* is given in the Contract Data. The obligation to reply within the relevant period is stated in clause 13.3.
Changing a decision	(7)	The *Service Manager* is able to change a decision made under the authority given to him in the contract, in the same way that he made the original decision.
Withholding acceptance	(8)	Various clauses state reasons why the *Service Manager* is entitled not to accept a submission or proposal from the *Contractor*. Rejection of a submission or proposal for reasons other than those stated is a compensation event.
Delayed tests or inspections	(9)	Testing and inspection work to be carried out by the *Service Manager* is stated in the Service Information. Under clause 40.5, the *Service Manager* is required to do this without causing unnecessary delay.
Change to Affected Property	(10)	A change to the Affected Property during the *service period* may affect the *Contractor*'s work in Providing the Service, and also the cost.
Materials, facilities etc. for tests	(11)	Under clause 40.2 the *Employer* is required to provide materials, facilities and samples for tests as stated in the Service Information.
Employer's risks	(12)	*Employer*'s risks are stated in clause 80.1.
Assumptions about compensation events	(13)	Under clause 61.6, the *Service Manager* may state assumptions to be used in assessing compensation events. If he later notifies corrections to these assumptions, the notification is a separate compensation event under clause 60.1(13).
Employer's breach of contract	(14)	This is an 'umbrella' clause to include breaches of contract by the *Employer* within the compensation event procedure.

Notifying compensation events   **61**

61.1   This procedure would normally apply to compensation events 1, 4, 7, 8 and 13 each of which is due to an action by the *Service Manager*. When the event occurs, the *Service Manager* notifies the *Contractor* and instructs him to submit quotations. Where the compensation even results from the *Contractor*'s fault or where quotations have already been submitted, quotations are not instructed. However, in order to avoid doubt in such cases, it is advisable that when the *Service Manager* notifies the compensation event, he should give his reason for not instructing quotations. The *Contractor* is required to act on the instruction or changed decision.

It is important that the *Service Manager* notifies such compensation events, without waiting for the *Contractor* to do so. If he does not so he will leave the *Employer* open to late claims from the *Contractor*, because the time-bar in clause 61.3 does not apply to these types of events.

61.2   This clause deals with the situation where the *Service Manager* is considering issuing an instruction or changing a decision but first requires to know what effect this would have on cost (for example, when he is considering a change to the *Service Information* (clause 60.1(1)). He has authority to instruct the *Contractor* to submit quotations as a first step.

61.3   This procedure would normally apply to the compensation events not covered by those in clause 61.1. These are events which arise from

- a failure by the *Employer*, *Service Manager* or Others to fulfil their obligations (compensation events 2, 3, 5, 6, 9, 11 and 14),
- the *Service Manager* withholding an acceptance for a reason not stated in the contract (compensation event 8) or
- a happening not caused by any Party (compensation event 10, 12).

It would also apply to an event which the *Service Manager* should have notified under clause 61.1 but did not do so. In such cases, the *Contractor* initiates the procedure by notifying the *Service Manager*.

To avoid having to deal with a compensation event long after it has occurred there is a time limit on notification by the *Contractor*. Failure to comply with this time limit "time-bars" the *Contractor* from any compensation for the event, unless the event is one which the *Service Manager* should have notified under clause 61.1.

61.4 This clause deals with the *Service Manager*'s response to the *Contractor*'s notification of compensation events under clause 61.3. It lists the four tests which the *Service Manager* applies to an event notified by the *Contractor* in order to decide whether or not to instruct the *Contractor* to submit quotations for its effect. If the *Service Manager* decides that the event does not pass any one of the tests, he notifies the *Contractor* and no further action is required unless the *Contractor* disputes the decision and refers it to the *Adjudicator* under the dispute resolution procedure.

In many circumstances, the *Service Manager* will be able to give his decision within a week of the *Contractor*'s notification. With more complicated events, a longer period will be desirable to ensure adequate time for a properly considered decision. Provision is made for such longer periods subject to the *Contractor*'s agreement.

The final paragraph of this clause protects the *Contractor* against a delay by the *Service Manager* in responding to the *Contractor*'s notification.

61.5 The *Service Manager* should include, in an instruction to submit quotations, his decision on whether or not the *Contractor* gave an early warning which an experienced contractor could have given. This is necessary to permit the application of the sanction in clause 63.6.

61.6 In some cases, the nature of a compensation event may be such that it is impossible to prepare a sufficiently accurate quotation, e.g. where the quantum of work involved cannot be decided until the work is started. In these cases, quotations are submitted on the basis of assumptions stated by the *Service Manager* in his instruction to the *Contractor*. If the assumptions later prove to be wrong, the *Service Manager*'s notification of their correction is a separate compensation event – clause 60.1(13).

Apart from this situation, the assessment of a compensation event cannot be revised – clause 65.2. The reason for this strict procedure is to motivate the Parties to decide the effects of a compensation event either before or soon after it occurs. Since each quotation includes due allowance for risk (clause 63.7), and the fact that the early warning procedure should minimise the effects of unexpected problems, the need for later review is minimal.

Quotations for **62**
compensation events 62.1 There may be several ways of adjusting plans for the work to deal with a compensation event and its consequences. The procedure in this clause enables the *Service Manager* to consider different options. For instance, it may be more beneficial to the *Employer* to have an additional service carried out quickly or at a more convenient time, but at a greater cost than might otherwise be the case. The clause also provides for the *Contractor* to submit quotations using methods other than those assumed in the *Service Manager*'s instruction. For instance, the *Contractor* may be able to use a specialised item of Equipment, the availability of which the *Service Manager* was unaware.

In priced Option A the cost of preparing quotations for a compensation event is specifically excluded from the assessment of that compensation event (clause 63.12). The *Contractor* should therefore allow for these costs in the *fee percentages* he provides in the Contract Data.

62.2 The use of the term 'quotations' is not the same as the normal use in commerce, i.e. the free submission of an offer. A build-up of each quotation is required to show its derivation. If re-planning of other work is affected, the quotation should include details of any alterations required to the Accepted Plan.

62.3   The time limits are intended to promote efficient management of the contract procedures. The four categories of reply by the *Service Manager* are listed. The third category may result from the *Service Manager* deciding not to proceed with a proposed change to the Service Information. This may happen when the cost of the change is too high or interference with the *Employer*'s activities too great. The *Service Manager* has absolute discretion on whether to proceed.

62.4   This procedure permits revision of quotations. In practice, this will usually follow discussion between the *Service Manager* and the *Contractor* on the details of the submitted quotations.

62.5   This provision permits extension of the time for submitting quotations. It would be used where consequences of a compensation event may be complex.

62.6   The procedure in this clause is designed to deal with a situation where the *Service Manager* does not reply within the time stated in the contract or a longer agreed time. Failure by the *Service Manager* to respond to a quotation, within the stated time results is 'deemed' acceptance.

Assessing compensation   **63**
events   63.1   Any appropriate rates in the Price List are to be used in assessing compensation events.

63.2   Compensation events which cannot be assessed under clause 63.1, are assessed on the basis of their effect on Defined Cost (either recorded cost of work already done or forecast of the cost of future work), plus the Fee.

Where the work to be done is changed, it is important that the assessment is based upon the change in forecast or recorded Defined Cost. This clause gives no authority for the price for the originally specified work to be deleted and for the forecast Defined Cost plus Fee of all work now required to be used for the basis of the new price.

If the Service Information originally included a piece of work (a) which is now to be replaced by a piece of work (b), the compensation event is assessed as the difference between the forecast Defined Cost for (a) and the forecast Defined Cost for (b), to which is added the Fee. The original price for (a) does not enter the assessment, and instead the assessment (plus or minus) is applied to that original price. Similarly if the effect of the compensation event is to delete a future item of work, the original price is not merely deleted. Instead the assessment is based upon the forecast Defined Cost plus Fee for that work, which is then applied to the original price to end up with a positive or negative figure.

Clause 63.2 pinpoints the date when there is a switch from recorded Defined Cost to forecast Defined Cost included in a quotation. This ensures that whoever is making the assessment of the compensation event, that assessment is based upon the same principles. Therefore neither the *Contractor* nor *Service Manager* can choose the switch date in order to suit their own purposes. Similarly the *Adjudicator* is also required to use this switch date when assessing compensation events.

For compensation events which the *Service Manager* should notify under clause 61.1, the switch date will be the date of the communication which led to the compensation event, not the date when the compensation event was notified by either the *Contractor* or *Service Manager*. For all other compensation events the switch date will be the date when the compensation event is notified.

These rules also apply to the situation where there is an instruction to submit a revised quotation under clauses 62.3 and 62.4. In that case the revised quotation will use the same switch date as the original quotation.

Assessment of compensation events is based on the pricing of the four components of Defined Cost listed in clause 11.2(5). This states how the Equipment element is priced.

63.3 An alternative method of assessing compensation events is by using the rates and prices in the Price List as a basis, but this can only be done by agreement between the *Service Manager* and *Contractor*.

63.4 The Prices can be reduced only where expressly permitted in the contract.

63.5 This clause restricts the rights of the Parties in assessing the effects of a compensation event.

63.6 The *Contractor*'s duty to give an early warning is stated in clause 16.1. This clause states the sanction to be applied if the *Contractor* fails to give early warning. It is possible that early warning could have allowed action to be taken which would have reduced costs and caused less interference with the *Employer*'s activities. It is important that the *Service Manager* notifies the *Contractor* of his decision that early warning should have been given (clause 61.5) so that the *Contractor* knows the correct basis for his assessment.

63.7 Allowance for risk must be included in forecasts of Defined Cost in the same way that the *Contractor* allows for risk when pricing his tender. The value of the allowance is greater when the work is uncertain and there is a high chance of a *Contractor*'s risk happening. It is least when the uncertainties are small and when the work is to be done using resources already available, whose output rates can be predicted fairly precisely.

63.8 This clause protects the *Employer* against inefficiency on the part of the *Contractor*.

63.9 This clause expresses the 'contra proferentem' rule, which interprets a clause containing an ambiguity or inconsistency against the party responsible for drafting the document in which it occurs.

The *Service Manager*'s **64**
assessments 64.1 The four circumstances in which the *Service Manager* assesses a compensation event are stated. They are all derived from some failure of the *Contractor*. In making his assessments, the *Service Manager* will be motivated to make a fair and reasonable assessment in the knowledge that the *Contractor* may refer the matter to the *Adjudicator*, who may change the assessment.

64.2 This clause provides the *Service Manager* with the same time to make his assessment as the *Contractor* was allowed for his assessment.

64.3 The procedure in this clause is designed to deal with a situation where the *Service Manager* does not assess a compensation event within the time stated in the contract or a longer agreed time. The *Contractor* may notify the *Service Manager* accordingly, which effectively provides the *Service Manager* with a two week 'period of grace' to respond. If this produces no action from the *Service Manager*, the quotation submitted by the *Contractor* is treated as having been accepted.

Implementing **65**
compensation events 65.1 This clause should be read in conjunction with clause 65.3 for Options A and C and clause 65.4 for Option E.

65.2 This clause emphasises the finality of the assessment of compensation events. If the records of resources on work actually carried out show that achieved Defined Cost is different from the forecast included in the accepted quotation or in the *Service Manager*'s assessment, the assessment is not changed.

MAIN OPTION CLAUSES

Option A: Priced contract with price list

Assessing compensation events **63**

63.12   The changed Price List which takes account of the effect of compensation events may be used for subsequent assessments of the PSPD.

Implementing compensation events **65**

65.3   See explanatory notes on clause 65.1.

Option C: Target contract with price list

Assessing compensation events **63**

63.12   The changed Price List which takes account of the effect of compensation events may be used for subsequent assessments of the PSPD.

Implementing compensation events **65**

65.3   See explanatory notes on clause 65.1.

Option E: Cost reimbursable contract

Implementing compensation events **65**

65.4   See explanatory notes on clause 65.1.

7 Use of equipment, Plant and Materials

CORE CLAUSES

The Parties' use of equipment, Plant and Materials **70**

70.1   This clause prohibits the *Contractor* from using equipment, Plant and Materials for his own purposes or for purposes other than for Providing the Service.

70.2   This requires the *Contractor* to return to the *Employer* at the end of the *service period* things which have been provided by the *Employer* for the *Contractor*'s use. If the Service Information so states, the *Employer* may take over from the *Contractor* at the end of the *service period* Equipment belonging to the *Contractor* and which he has used to Provide the Service.

8 Risks and insurance

CORE CLAUSES

Where Option X18 (limitation of liability) is included in the contract, much of the following commentary will be modified by that Option.

It is important to recognise the distinction between the various types of risk and which party bears them. Risks of loss of or physical damage to property or of personal injury or death, which are usually insurable risks, are quite separate from general, legal or financial risks.

Section 8 deals with the general, legal and insurable risks of loss, damage, injury or death and what insurances are required to cover them. The risks which could result in loss, damage, injury or death, if they happen, are allocated to either the *Employer* or the *Contractor.*

Financial risks are dealt with in other parts of the contract, such as under the compensation event procedure in Section 6. For example, the *Employer* carries the financial risk for additional work instructed under clause 60.1(1), but the risk in carrying it out remains with the *Contractor.*

Conversely, the *Contractor* carries the financial risk of doing work which he has priced in the contract including the insurance requirements under clause 83.1.

Employer's risks 80
80.1 The *Employer*'s risks are stated in clause 80.1. There are five main categories of *Employer*'s risks.

The first is the *Employer*'s risks relating to his use of the Affected Property, his own general or legal responsibilities and faults in his design. For liabilities which might arise from design faults the *Employer* should either insure the risk by a professional indemnity policy if the design is by his own resources or ensure that it is covered (e.g. under the NEC Professional Services Contract) if an external consultant is engaged to do the design work.

The second category relating to items supplied to the *Contractor* is at the risk of the *Employer* up to the point of their handover to the *Contractor* or a Subcontractor. Any insurance cover for these should be either under the *Employer*'s own loss or damage policy or the insurances of Others (as defined in clause 11.2(9)) until the *Contractor* or Subcontractor has received and accepted the Plant and Materials concerned.

The third category of *Employer*'s risk is the loss of or damage to the Affected Property, Plant and Materials caused by outside influences beyond the control of the Parties. This risk is limited to what can be regarded as the *Employer*'s property. The *Contractor* carries the risk of loss of or damage to his property from any of these causes.

The fourth category of *Employer*'s risk is that of loss of or damage to any Equipment, Plant and Materials retained by the *Employer* after termination.

The last category of the *Employer*'s risks provides for him to carry additional risks. These must be clearly stated in the Contract Data. An important example of where the *Employer* might wish to carry an additional risk or limit the *Contractor*'s risk is in relation to the Affected Property, other than the *Employer*'s property.

If the *Contractor* and the *Employer* share a risk then the *Contractor* must ensure that his insurances are adequate at least up to the limit of his risk.

Another example would be for equipment made available to the *Contractor* by the *Employer* for which the *Employer* preferred to retain direct control and hence risk. A vital distinction must then be recognised between the equipment which concerns the *Employer* and the Equipment (note the capital 'E' for Equipment in the second classification of insurance in the Insurance Table) as defined in clause 11.2(7). Thus the risk of loss of or damage to equipment under this example is an *Employer*'s risk but loss of or damage to defined Equipment is a *Contractor*'s risk.

The *Contractor*'s risks   **81**

81.1   The *Contractor*'s risks are defined as all the risks which are not identified in clause 80.1 as being carried by the *Employer*. The *Contractor*'s risks include those as stated in the insurance clauses even when such risk is covered by insurance procured by the *Employer*. This aspect is explained more fully in the notes for clause 86.2.

Indemnity   **82**

82.1   Under this clause each Party indemnifies the other for events which are at his risk.

82.2   Provision is made for the liability of a Party to be reduced on a proportional basis if events at the risk of the other Party contributed to the event.

Insurance cover   **83**

83.1   This clause requires the *Contractor* to take out insurance cover. Major multi-discipline employers may prefer to arrange all or some of this insurance themselves, in view of the large number and size of contracts in which they invest. In such cases, insurers are likely to take a much greater interest in the running of the contract as the *Contractor* is no longer motivated to minimise claims. If the *Employer* wishes to effect his own insurance, the details should be given in the Contract Data. Otherwise, the events and extent of cover to be effected by the *Contractor* are as shown in the Insurance Table and detailed in the Contract Data.

Insurance of the *Employer*'s property and Equipment covers only the *Contractor*'s risks. It is for the *Employer* to decide whether or not he wishes to take out insurance cover for his own risks. It is important in all cases to check that the terms of any standard policy comply with the requirements of the contract.

Insurance of Equipment, and Plant and Materials is on a value indemnity basis. This is particularly relevant to insurance of Equipment as it means that cover is for replacement with equipment of similar age and condition rather than on a 'new-for-old' basis.

With regard to the fifth event in the Insurance Table, employers in many countries are required by law to insure employees for personal injury and death.

The *Service Manager* and the *Contractor* must ensure that the policies and certificates are in the joint names of the *Employer* and the *Contractor* including for those insurances procured by the *Employer* for those matters at the *Contractor*'s risk.

Insurance policies   **84**

84.1   The *Contractor*'s insurers or insurance brokers are required to provide a certificate stating that the requisite insurances under the contract are in force.

84.2   The purpose of waiver of subrogation rights is to prevent insurers taking action against the *Employer*'s personnel, for example after having paid money to the *Contractor* in settlement of a claim by him.

84.3   The Parties must comply with the terms of the insurance policies as not to do so may invalidate the insurance in part or in whole and incur the Parties in substantial risk.

84.4 Careful consideration should be given by the *Employer* and the *Contractor* to the amounts for deductibles. Deductibles, sometimes known as excesses, represent the amount of liability retained by the insured. By this means, the insured shares the exposure to risk with the insurer.

The amount of the deductible affects the level of premium which the insured must pay. Reasons for applying deductibles in insurance policies include

- decrease in level of premiums,
- elimination of administration costs of processing a large number of small claims,
- involving the insured in retaining some liability by sharing the risks and thus encouraging him to take more care in avoiding loss or damage and
- reducing the risk assumed by the insurer to a limit which he can bear.

Employers who enter 'nil' against the deductibles in the Contract Data are likely to pay very high level premiums.

If the *Contractor* does not insure **85**

85.1 This clause enables the *Employer* to take out the relevant insurances in the event that the *Contractor* fails to do so at the time and for the periods stated in the contract. Appropriate adjustments are then made to the amounts certified by the *Service Manager*.

Insurance by the *Employer* **86**

86.1 In certain circumstances it may be more appropriate and convenient for the *Employer* to effect some of the joint name insurances which, under the standard conditions, are to be taken out by the *Contractor*.

86.2 Whilst the *Contractor* is entitled to rely upon the *Employer* providing the insurances as stated in the Contract Data, it is important that the *Contractor* recognises that his risks include those shown in the Insurance Table. Consequently, even if such insurances are effected by the *Employer*, the *Contractor* should satisfy himself as to the adequacy of the policy and cover. The *Contractor* should inform the *Service Manager* of any discrepancy between the *Employer*-provided insurances as stated in the Contract Data and the *Employer*-provided insurances as actually given and ask for a policy amendment.

86.3 If the *Employer*

- fails to effect the insurances which the Contract Data states he is to provide or
- provides insurances which do not comply with the Contract Data,

the *Contractor* may procure additional insurance to top up any shortfall he considers exists in these insurances. The *Employer* will then either pay the insurers directly or the *Contractor* will be reimbursed.

9 Termination

CORE CLAUSES

This section describes the circumstances under which the Parties may terminate the contract and the subsequent procedures on termination.

Termination 90

90.1   Both the *Employer* and *Contractor* have rights to terminate the *Contractor*'s obligations under the contract in certain circumstances. This termination does not terminate the contract itself. The Party wishing to terminate initiates the procedure by notifying the *Service Manager* and giving his reasons for terminating. If satisfied that there are valid contractual grounds for termination, the *Service Manager* issues a termination certificate promptly.

90.2   Only the *Employer* has a right of termination entirely at his discretion, i.e. without one of the reasons listed in R1 to R21. The *Contractor* can terminate only for one of the reasons listed in the Termination Table. For convenience, the reasons are given an identification reference and are fully described in clause 91. If the *Employer* wishes to terminate for a reason other than those in R1 to R21, he should state this in notifying the *Service Manager* under clause 90.1.

The procedures to be followed and the amount due to the *Contractor* are generally related to the reasons for terminating, although some are independent of the reasons.

90.3   The procedures are given in clause 92.

90.4   Details of the amount due on termination are given in clause 93 in conjunction with the Termination Table. The *Service Manager* is required to assess the amount due so that he can certify the final payment within thirteen weeks. Payment is to be made within a further three weeks.

Reasons for termination 91

91.1   The terminology of bankruptcy law varies from country to country. The terms used in this clause are those current in English law but the clause allows for equivalents in other jurisdictions. Termination may follow the bankruptcy, etc., of either the *Contractor* or the *Employer*.

91.2   The four week period of grace is provided so that the *Contractor* has the opportunity to correct the default. Notification should be issued to the *Contractor* and usually copied to the *Employer*. If after four weeks the *Contractor* has not corrected the default, the *Service Manager* would, by implication, need to advise the *Employer* of the position so that the *Employer* can exercise his right if he wishes. The *Contractor* may have started to make amends but not fully corrected the default after the four week period. In this case, the *Employer* will need to decide whether or not he wishes to proceed to termination.

Reason R11 applies only to a substantial breach of the *Contractor*'s obligations. Minor breaches are insufficient grounds for the serious step of termination.

The guarantee in Option X4 and the bond in Option X13 are both to be provided within certain times. This clause effectively extends those times by four weeks.

Subcontracting of work before acceptance by the *Service Manager* (R13) is breach of clause 26.2. However, the right to termination only arises when substantial work is subcontracted before acceptance of the Subcontractor.

91.3   Both of these reasons include the word 'substantially' since minor defaults of this nature would not be sufficient grounds for termination. The right to termination for breach of a health and safety regulation is additional to any sanctions which may exist under the applicable law.

91.4 Late payment entitles the payee to interest under clause 51.2. The right to termination, however, only arises if payment by the *Employer* of an amount due to the *Contractor* is delayed beyond 11 weeks after the date it was due to be paid. This right can only be exercised by the *Contractor*.

91.5 In the event of a national emergency, such as declaration of war, a government often legislates to deal with existing contracts.

91.6 These reasons apply to instructions which relate to substantial or all work. Judgement is needed to interpret what constitutes substantial work. Procedures and payment depend on which Party was responsible for the default which led to the instruction. R20 provides for an instruction which resulted from the default of neither Party.

Procedures on termination 92

92.2 Under procedure P2, the *Employer*'s right to enforce assignment of the benefits of a subcontract will be subject to the terms of the subcontract. In certain cases, a new contract (novation) may be necessary.

Procedure P3 is particularly useful to an *Employer* where there are substantial items of Equipment involved or other major temporary works.

Payment on termination 93

93.1 The amounts listed in this clause (A1) are due whatever the reason for the termination.

Defined Cost reasonably incurred in expectation of completing the provision of the Service, should include costs which the *Contractor* can show have not been recovered within the normal amount due.

93.2 These amounts (A2 to A4) depend on the particular grounds of termination. Generally, where termination occurs because of the *Contractor*'s default, the *Contractor* is not reimbursed the cost of removing his Equipment. He must also pay the *Employer*'s additional costs for completing the whole of the *service*, representing at least some of the damages which the *Employer* suffers arising from the *Contractor*'s breach of contract.

MAIN OPTION CLAUSES

Option C: Target contract with Price List

Payment on termination 93

93.3 This clause allows for an assessment of the *Contractor*'s share at termination. It provides details of the figures to be used for the Prices, and also the Price for Services Provided to Date, in calculating the *Contractor*'s share.

DISPUTE RESOLUTION

Dispute resolution Option W1

This Option should be selected whenever the United Kingdom Housing Grants, Construction and Regeneration Act 1996 as amended by the Local Democracy, Economic Development and Construction Act 2009 does not apply to the contract in question.

It is the intention that disputes should be referred to and resolved by the *Adjudicator*. If either Party is dissatisfied with the *Adjudicator*'s decision and wishes to pursue the matter further, he is free to refer it to arbitration or the courts, whichever is identified as the *tribunal* in the Contract Data.

It is important for the Parties to understand that both dispute resolution processes should only be used after attempts at negotiations have failed. They should not be seen as an alternative to the Parties reaching agreement on their disputes, either through informal negotiation, or via other more formal non-binding processes such as mediation or conciliation. Such negotiations will usually need to take place within a short time period if Option W1 is used, because of the limited time available to refer a dispute to the *Adjudicator* in that Option. However the Parties are free to agree to extend the time limits set out in W1, in accordance with clause W1.3(2), if they feel that more time

is needed for resolving the dispute. If either the notification or the referral is not made within the time stated or extended by agreement, the Parties may no longer dispute the matter. Option W2 allows a dispute to be referred to the *Adjudicator* at any time, and therefore the Parties may take the time they wish to attempt to reach agreement.

Dispute resolution **W1**

W1.1   Disputes are to be dealt with by adjudication in the first instance.

The *Adjudicator* W1.2 The person appointed as *Adjudicator* is named in part one of the Contract
(1)   Data. He is to be appointed jointly by the Parties using the NEC Adjudicator's Contract (one of the documents of the NEC family of standard contracts published by Thomas Telford, London). His fees and expenses are shared equally between the Parties to a dispute, regardless of his decision, unless otherwise agreed.

The *Adjudicator* should be a person with experience of the kind of services required of the *Contractor* and who occupies or has occupied a senior position dealing with similar dispute problems. He should be able to understand the point of view of both *Employer* and *Contractor* and to judge the required level of skill, and be able to act impartially.

(2)   The obligation of impartiality is fundamental to the role of the *Adjudicator*. The duty is repeated in the NEC Adjudicator's Contract. The *Adjudicator*'s status is different from that of an arbitrator.

(3)   The *Adjudicator* is appointed jointly by the *Employer* and the *Contractor* for the contract. The *Employer* should insert his choice of *Adjudicator* in part one of the Contract Data. If the *Contractor* does not agree with the choice, a suitable person will be the subject of discussion and agreement before the Contract Date. Alternatively, the *Employer* may propose a list of acceptable names, and the *Contractor* may be asked to select one of them to be *Adjudicator*. Some *Employers* may prefer the *Contractor* to propose suitable names.

Where an *Adjudicator* has not been named in the Contract Data, this clause describes the procedure for appointing one. The procedure also applies where a replacement adjudicator is needed in the event that the named *Adjudicator* has resigned or is unable to act. In the United Kingdom there are several *Adjudicator nominating bodies*, who are able to appoint a suitable person to act as *Adjudicator*.

Any existing disputes on which the original *Adjudicator* has not made a decision are automatically referred to the replacement adjudicator. It is important that the Parties ensure that the replacement adjudicator receives all the relevant information. The time stated in the contract for supply of information then runs from the time of appointment of the replacement adjudicator.

If a need arises for a temporary replacement adjudicator (e.g. during the *Adjudicator*'s holiday), the Parties should agree a temporary appointment.

(5)   It is important that the person appointed as *Adjudicator* is protected from legal actions by the Parties and others.

The adjudication W1.3 This clause requires that any of the four categories of dispute listed in the
(1)   Adjudication Table is referred to the *Adjudicator*. Time limits are provided for notification of the dispute to the other Party and for reference to the *Adjudicator*.

(2)   The Parties are barred from referring a dispute to the *Adjudicator* or the *tribunal* outside the stated time limits.

(3)   It is important that the *Adjudicator* has all the relevant information to enable him to reach a decision. The Parties are required to submit all information supporting their case within four weeks of the first submission to the *Adjudicator*, or greater agreed period.

(4)   Where a dispute which affects services being carried out by a Subcontractor arises and which may constitute a dispute between the *Contractor* and Subcontractor as well as between the *Contractor* and the *Employer*, there is provision

for the matter to be resolved between the three Parties by the *Adjudicator* named in this contract. This prevents the dispute being dealt with by different adjudicators who may make different decisions. This does mean, however, that the adjudicator named in the subcontract will not be used for the dispute under that subcontract, and the Subcontractor will be obliged to use an *Adjudicator* he has not previously agreed to. It would be helpful if the *Adjudicator*'s name is included in the subcontract documents so that Subcontractors have prior knowledge of the identity of the *Adjudicator* in the main contract.

(5) Although the *Adjudicator* is empowered to review and revise any action or inaction of the *Employer*, the Parties are not permitted to widen the dispute to include other disputes which might have occurred after the original submission. The *Adjudicator* has wide powers under this clause. He may seek information himself in addition to information submitted by the Parties.

(6) It is important that copies of the communications sent to the *Adjudicator* are sent to the other Party so that each Party is aware of the other Party's case.

(7), (8) & (9) The *Adjudicator* in notifying his decision is required to state reasons for his decision and also to include his assessment of additional cost and delay as appropriate. Pending settlement of the dispute, the Parties proceed with their duties under the contract.

In complex disputes and for other valid reasons the *Adjudicator* may require a period greater than the four weeks stated. An extension of the period requires the agreement of the Parties. If such agreement is not forthcoming and the *Adjudicator* cannot or for some other reason does not notify his decision within the four week period, either Party may refer the dispute to the *tribunal* under clause W1.4(3).

(10) A valid decision by the *Adjudicator* is enforceable in the courts. The decision is also final unless within four weeks the dissatisfied Party has notified his intention to refer the dispute to the *tribunal* (clause W1.4(2)).

Review by the *tribunal* W1.4 (1) Initially the *Employer*, and by acceptance also the *Contractor* and Subcontractor, will select the method of final and binding dispute resolution. It can be either arbitration or litigation in the appropriate court.

If arbitration is chosen, the entry in the Contract Data against the *tribunal* is 'arbitration', together with the arbitration procedure proposed for the conduct of the arbitration and other details (clause W1.4(5)).

If litigation is chosen, appropriate entries must be made for the jurisdiction chosen. In England and Wales, the *tribunal* might be 'trial by a judge sitting as such in the High Court of Justice in London'. Advice should be taken, however, on the appropriate entry to provide for the jurisdiction intended.

(2) A dispute cannot be referred to arbitration or litigation unless it has been referred to the *Adjudicator*. A time limit is given for notification of intention to refer the matter to the *tribunal*, after which the *Adjudicator*'s decision will be final and no further notification of intended reference to the *tribunal* may be made. If the adjudication involves three Parties – i.e. a subcontractor is joined in the adjudication – the dispute resolution by the *tribunal* will also involve all three parties.

(3) A dispute may be referred to the *tribunal* where the *Adjudicator* has failed to notify his decision in time, as well as where a dissatisfied Party wishes to take the matter further.

Dispute resolution Option W2 This Option should be selected whenever the United Kingdom Housing Grants, Construction and Regeneration Act 1996 as amended by the Local Democracy, Economic Development and Construction Act 2009 (the Act) applies to the contract in question.

It is the intention that disputes should be referred to and resolved by the *Adjudicator*. If either Party is dissatisfied with the *Adjudicator*'s decision and wishes to pursue the matter further, he is free to refer it to arbitration or the

courts, whichever is identified as the *tribunal* in the Contract Data. The Parties may deal with the dispute by other means if they agree to do so.

Dispute resolution **W2**

W2.1
(1)

Disputes are to be dealt with by adjudication in the first instance. The phrase 'at any time' is a requirement of the Act. The only limit to this time is the limitation period for the contract. This means that disputes arising several years after the *Contractor* has completed his work may be submitted to the *Adjudicator.*

(2)

Generally, time periods in the TSC are stated in weeks. In Option W2 and the Act, time periods are in days, which means that 'day' must be defined. The definition in this clause is as in the Act. Days include Saturdays and Sundays.

The *Adjudicator* W2.2
(1)

The person appointed as *Adjudicator* is named in part one of the Contract Data. He is to be appointed jointly by the Parties using the NEC Adjudicator's Contract (one of the NEC family of standard contracts published by Thomas Telford, London).

The A*djudicator* should be a person with experience of the kind of *services* required of the *Contractor* and who occupies or has occupied a senior position dealing with similar dispute problems. He should be able to understand the point of view of both *Employer* and *Contractor* and to judge the required level of competence, and be able to act impartially.

(2)

The obligation of impartiality is fundamental to the role of *Adjudicator.* The duty is repeated in the NEC Adjudicator's Contract. The *Adjudicator*'s status is different from that of an arbitrator.

(3)

The *Adjudicator* is appointed jointly by the *Employer* and the *Contractor* for the contract. The *Employer* should insert his choice of *Adjudicator* in part one of the Contract Data. If the *Contractor* does not agree with the choice, a suitable person will be the subject of discussion and agreement before the Contract Date. Alternatively, the *Employer* may propose a list of acceptable names and the *Contractor* may be asked to select one of them to be *Adjudicator.* Some *Employer*s may prefer the *Contractor* to propose suitable names.

Where an *Adjudicator* has not been named in the Contract Data, this clause describes the procedure for appointing one. The procedure also applies where a replacement adjudicator is needed in the event that the named *Adjudicator* is unable to act. In the United Kingdom there are several *Adjudicator nominating bodies,* who are able to appoint a suitable person as *Adjudicator.*

(4)

Any existing disputes on which the original *Adjudicator* has not made a decision are automatically referred to the replacement adjudicator. It is important that the Parties ensure that the replacement adjudicator receives all relevant information. The time stated in the contract for supply of information then runs from the time of appointment of the replacement adjudicator.

If a need arises for a temporary replacement adjudicator (e.g. during the *Adjudicator*'s holiday), the Parties should agree a temporary appointment.

(5)

It is important that the person appointed as *Adjudicator* is protected from legal actions by the Parties and others. It is also a requirement of the Act.

The adjudication W2.3
(1)

The Party wishing to refer the dispute for adjudication initiates the procedure by giving a notice to the other Party, with a copy to the *Adjudicator.* The procedure also confirms or otherwise whether the *Adjudicator* is to proceed with the adjudication.

The time periods in this clause and clause W2.2(3) are designed to ensure that an adjudicator is appointed within seven days as required by the Act.

(2)

It is important that the *Adjudicator* has all the relevant information to enable him to reach his decision. The Parties are required to submit all information supporting their case within fourteen days of the submission of the dispute to the *Adjudicator,* or greater agreed period.

(3) Where a dispute which affects services being carried out by a Subcontractor arises and which may constitute a dispute between the *Contractor* and the Subcontractor as well as between the *Contractor* and the *Employer*, there is provision for the matter to be resolved between the three Parties by the *Adjudicator* named in this contract. This prevents the dispute being dealt with by different adjudicators who may make different decisions. This does mean, however, that the adjudicator named in the subcontract will not be used for the dispute under that subcontract, and the Subcontractor will be obliged to use an *Adjudicator* he has not previously agreed to. It would be helpful if the *Adjudicator*'s name is included in the subcontract documents so that the Subcontractor has prior knowledge of the identity of the *Adjudicator* in the main contract. Because of the timing requirements of the Act, this process will only be practical with the agreement of the Subcontractor, which has been made a requirement.

(4) Although the *Adjudicator* is empowered to review and revise any action or inaction of the *Employer*, the Parties are not permitted, unless agreed by the Parties and the *Adjudicator,* to widen the dispute to include other disputes which might have occurred after the original submission. The *Adjudicator* has wide powers under this clause. He may seek information himself in addition to information submitted by the Parties.

(5) It is important that any delay caused by a Party does not delay or stop the adjudication. Thus, where a Party does not comply with the *Adjudicator*'s instructions, the adjudication continues. This would also apply where a Party refuses to take part in the adjudication.

(6) It is important that copies of the communications sent to the *Adjudicator* are sent to the other Party so that each Party is aware of the other Party's case.

(8) The *Adjudicator* in notifying his decision is required to state reasons for his decision and also to include his assessment of additional cost and delay as appropriate.

In complex disputes and for other valid reasons the *Adjudicator* may require a period greater than the twenty-eight days stated. An extension of fourteen days may be granted if the referring Party agrees, or other period if both Parties agree.

The *Adjudicator* has the power to decide how to allocate his fees and expenses between the Parties. This clause, which is required by the Act, means that the Parties have agreed to implement the provision in the NEC Adjudicator's Contract allowing the Parties to agree that these fees and expenses will not be shared equally.

(11) A valid decision by the *Adjudicator* is enforceable in the courts. The decision is also final unless within the relevant time the dissatisfied Party has notified his intention to refer the dispute to the *tribunal* under clause W2.4(2).

(12) Once the *Adjudicator* has made his decision and notified it to the Parties his role in the dispute would normally be over. This clause gives him the right to subsequently correct a clerical or typographical error which has arisen by accident or by omission, as required by the Act.

Review by the *tribunal* W2.4 (1) The *Employer* should insert in the Contract Data the *tribunal* that will decide a dispute if either Party does not accept the *Adjudicator*'s decision. The choice will normally be either arbitration or the courts. An individual person should not be named.

(3) The *tribunal* has wide powers to settle the dispute and is not tied to a decision or action of the *Service Manager*. Referral of a dispute to the *tribunal* should not be regarded as an appeal against the *Adjudicator*'s decision. Thus, the Parties may rely on new evidence and submissions that were not put before the *Adjudicator*.

(4) Standard arbitration procedures generally deal with appointment of arbitrators, replacement arbitrators and time limits. Standard procedures for civil engineering works in the United Kingdom include those published by the Institution of Civil Engineers, and for building works those published by the Joint Contracts Tribunal (JCT).

SECONDARY OPTION CLAUSES

Option X1: Price adjustment for inflation (used only with Options A and C)

In the case of Options A and C, the *Employer* should decide how the risk of inflation is to be allocated. If he decides to accept this risk himself, he should include Option X1. Without Option X1, the contract is firm price and the *Contractor* carries the risk of inflationary increases in the cost of labour, Plant and Materials, etc.

For Option E, the cost reimbursable contract, the *Employer* already carries this risk since payments are of recorded Defined Cost. These are 'current costs' and automatically include for price increases occurring after the contract was signed.

A target contract requires the *Employer* to decide whether to use the price adjustment for inflation. It is applied to the rates and prices in the Price List so that the total of the Prices can be fairly compared with Defined Cost and Fee for calculating the *Contractor*'s share.

Defined terms **X1**

X1.1   The source of the published priced indices to be used should be identified in part one of the Contract Data, together with the proportions of the total value of the *service* to be linked to the index for each category. Allowance is made for a non-adjustable portion, which represents the portion for which the *Contractor* carries the risk of inflation. The non-adjustable portion is usually a small proportion of the total factor – a maximum of 10% is normally considered reasonable. The total of the proportions should be unity.

Also entered in the Contract Data is the *base date*, which should normally be four to six weeks before the latest date for submitting tenders.

Price Adjustment Factor X1.2   Quite often, provisional index figures are published and these are corrected at a later date. This clause requires re-calculation using final figures where these are different from provisional figures.

Compensation events X1.3   Compensation events are assessed under clauses 63.1 and 63.2. Where only quantities of work are affected by the compensation event, the rates in the Price List are used (clause 63.1). These rates are at *base date* level. Other compensation events are assessed as the effect of the event on Defined Cost – either recorded past cost or forecast future cost, or a combination of the two. This assessment will be done using prices current at the date when the assessment is done. Clause X1.3 has the effect of reducing current Defined Cost to *base date* levels so that changes to the Prices for compensation events are made in *base date* terms.

When assessments of the amount due are made, the Price for Services Provided to Date (PSPD) will be adjusted for inflation under clause X1.4 or X1.5 as applicable.

If Option X1 is not included in a contract, the contract is fixed price with respect to inflation. However, compensation events are still assessed under clauses 63.1 and 63.2, which in the general case will be a mixture of current costs and *base date* costs. Tenderers will need to consider the allowance for inflation in the rates in the Price List as these may be used for assessing compensation events.

Price adjustment X1.4
Option A

'Each amount due' is the total to date and only the change in the amount due is payable (clause 51.1). Thus the total of the three bullet points listed in clause X1.4 represents the total amount in respect of price adjustment up to the date of each assessment.

Example

Assume the increase in the PSPD in a monthly assessment is £5,000 and the Price Adjustment Factor (PAF) is 0.05 (i.e. 5% inflation since the *base date*). The calculation for the first bullet point in clause X1.4 is:

$$£5,000 \times 0.05 = £250$$

The sum of £250, plus the total of the sums resulting from the same calculation in previous months, plus any correcting amount resulting from the third bullet point, is the amount for price adjustment included in the total amount due.

Price adjustment X1.5
Option C

Adjustment for inflation for a target contract is necessary only for the calculation of the *Contractor*'s share and not the monthly payment of the amount due. This arises because the Price for Services Provided to Date (PSPD) is the Defined Cost plus Fee. Defined Cost is current cost and automatically includes any inflation occurring since the *base date*. However, since the *Contractor*'s share is calculated from the difference between the Prices and the PSPD, the two must be compatible in terms of allowance for inflation. The total of the Prices is derived from the Price List, and it is this which must be adjusted for inflation.

The first of the two bullet points in clause X1.5 determines the inflationary component of the increase in the PSPD since the last assessment (normally the previous month).

Example

Assume the increase in the PSPD for the assessment is £5,000 and the PAF is 0.05%. The calculation for the first bullet point in clause X1.5 is:

$$PSPD \times \frac{PAF}{1 + PAF} = \frac{PSPD \times PAF}{1 + PAF}$$

$$\text{i.e.} \quad \frac{5,000 \times 0.05}{1.05} = 238.1$$

The sum of £238.1, plus any correcting amount resulting from the second bullet point, is the price adjustment amount for the assessment and is added to the total of the Prices. The result of this calculation at each assessment is added to the total of the Prices to maintain comparability with the Price for Services Provided to Date when the *Contractor*'s share is calculated.

X2: Changes in the law

Changes in the law X2
X2.1

This clause removes from the *Contractor* the risk of changes in the law which occur after the Contract Date. In certain countries, such changes can have a dramatic effect on the *Contractor*'s costs and on his ability to make progress. Also, in the cost of long service periods of, say, ten years duration, changes in the law may constitute a significant risk. Only changes which affect the *Contractor*'s costs are included. Thus changes of law affecting the following are not compensation events.

- Income tax or any other tax paid by employees.
- Corporation tax or any other charges on profits.

Changes of law affecting the following would be compensation events.

- Employment tax paid by the *Contractor*.
- Import duties.
- Customs payments.

For the purposes of this clause, law would include a national or state statute, ordinance, decree, regulation (including building or safety regulations) and a by-law of a local or other duly constituted authority or other delegated legislation.

The *Contractor* may notify the *Service Manager* of a compensation event under this Option using the procedure in clause 61.3. He is most likely to do this when a change in the law has the effect of increasing the cost to him of Providing the Service. However, the clause is reciprocal in the sense that the *Employer* gains the benefit of a change in the law which reduces costs.

X3: Multiple currencies (used only with Option A)

Provision for multiple currencies in Option C is made in clause 50.6 and in Option E in clause 50.7.

Multiple currencies X3

X3.1 This Option is used when it is intended that payment to the *Contractor* should be made in more than one currency and that the risk of exchange rate changes should be carried by the *Employer*. The effect is that the *Contractor* is protected from the currency *exchange rate* changes which take place after a fixed date as they affect designated items or activities of the *Contractor*'s work.

If an item or activity is to be paid for by the *Employer* in the *currency of the contract* and the *Contractor* chooses to pay for it, or part of it, in another currency, the *Contractor* carries the risk of changes in the *exchange rate*. Payment to the *Contractor* is not affected.

If, however, the total of the Prices at the Contract Date, which will be expressed in the *currency of the contract*, includes items identified as to be paid by the *Employer* to the *Contractor* in another currency, the *Employer* takes the risk of any movement in the exchange rate after the date of the published exchange rates stated in the Contract Data. This is achieved by listing the items in the Contract Data and fixing the *exchange rate* to be used for each currency relative to the *currency of the contract*. This ensures that the *Contractor* is paid the amount of the other currency which he has quoted for the item.

X4: Parent company guarantee

Parent company guarantee X4

X4.1 Where a parent company guarantee is required by the *Employer* it should be provided by the Contract Date. If that is not achieved, a four week limit is provided as a fall-back. Failure to provide the guarantee within this period entitles the *Service Manager* to notify the default under clause 91.2. If the *Contractor* does not provide the guarantee within a further four weeks, the *Employer* is entitled to terminate. The form of guarantee should be included in the Service Information in part one of the Contract Data. If the *Employer* wishes specific provision for the *Contractor* to price the guarantee separately in his tender, an appropriate item should be included in the Price List.

X12: Partnering

This Option is used for partnering between more than two parties working on the same project or projects or on the provision of services. The Option is included in all NEC contracts which each party has with the body which is paying for the work or service. The parties who have this Option included in their contracts are intended to make up the partnering team. The Partnering Option does not, however, create a multi-party contract.

The content of the Option is derived from the *Guide to Project Team Partnering* published by the Construction Industry Council (CIC). The requirements of the CIC document that are not already in the NEC contracts are covered by this Option.

The purpose of the Option is to establish the NEC family as an effective contract basis for multi-party partnering. By linking this Option to other bi-party contracts, the NEC can be used

- for partnering for any number of projects and services,
- internationally,
- for projects and services of any technical composition and
- as far down the supply chain as required.

Parties must recognise that by entering into a contract which includes Option X12, they will be undertaking responsibilities additional to those in the basic NEC contract.

A dispute (or difference) between Partners who do not have a contract between themselves is resolved by the Core Group. This is the Group that manages the conduct of the Partners in accordance with the Partnering Information. If the Core Group is unable to resolve the issue, then it is resolved under the procedure of the Partners' individual contracts, either directly or indirectly with the *Client* who will always be involved at some stage in the contractual chain. The *Client* may seek to have issues on all contracts dealt with simultaneously.

The Partnering Option does not include direct remedies between non-contracting Partners to recover losses suffered by one of them caused by failure of the other. These remedies remain available in each Partner's individual contract, but their existence will encourage the parties to compromise any differences that arise. This applies to all levels of the supply chain, as a Contractor who is a Partner retains the responsibility for actions of a subcontractor who is a Partner. The final sanction against any Partner who fails to act as stated in the Partnering Option is for the Partner who employed them not to invite them to partner again.

There are many scenarios possible in which the Partnering Option may be used. The NEC family of contracts with the Partnering Option is sufficiently flexible to deal with them. For example, the contract may be an Engineering and Construction Contract or an Engineering and Construction Short Contract for a project. It may involve also a Professional Services Contract. Later, a Term Service Contract may cover maintenance of the asset created by the project and provision of other services for the *Client*.

Identified and defined terms

X12.1 (1) The point at which someone becomes a Partner is when his Own Contract (which includes the Partnering Option) comes into existence. They should be named in the Schedule of Partners, and their representative identified.

(3) Not every Partner is a member of the Core Group.

(5) There are two options for subcontractor partners. Either the amount payable cascades down if the schedule allocates the same bonus/cost to the main contractor and subcontractor, or the main contractor absorbs the bonus/cost and does not pass it on.

Working together X12.3 The Core Group organises and holds meetings. It produces and distributes
(5) records of each meeting, which include agreed actions. Instructions from the
Core Group are issued in accordance with the Partner's Own Contract. The
Core Group may invite other Partners or people to attend a meeting of the
Core Group.

(8) The Partners should give advice and assistance when asked, and in addition
whenever they identify something that would be helpful to another Partner.

(9) A subcontractor may be a Partner, but the general policy on this should be
decided at the beginning of the project or service contract. The Core Group
should advise the Contractor at the outset if a subcontractor is to be asked to
be a Partner. A subcontractor who the Core Group decides should be a Partner
should not be appointed if he is unwilling to be a Partner.

Incentives X12.4 If one Partner lets the others down for a particular project or service by poor
(1) performance, then all lose their bonus for that target. If the *Employer* tries to
prevent a target being met, he is in breach of clause 10.1.

There can be more than one Key Performance Indicator (KPI) for each partner.
KPIs may apply to one Partner, to several Partners or to all Partners.

Example of a KPI

KPI	Highways licensing of skips
Target	Skip applications decided within 3 days
Measurement	Number of applications decided.
Amount	Main contractor £5 per application
	Subcontractor £30 per application

(2) The *Client* should consult with the other Partners before adding a KPI. The
effect on subcontracted work should be noted. Adding a KPI to work which is
subcontracted can involve a change to the KPI for a subcontractor.

Option X13: Performance bond

Performance bond **X13**
X13.1 Where a performance bond is required by the *Employer* the ideal is that it
should be provided by the Contract Date. If that is not achieved, a four week
limit is provided as a fall-back. Failure to provide the bond within this period
entitles the *Service Manager* to notify the default under clause 91.2. If the
Contractor does not provide the bond within a further four weeks, the *Employer*
is entitled to terminate. The form of the performance bond should be included
in the Service Information and the amount of the bond should be stated in the
Contract Data. If the *Employer* wishes the *Contractor* to price the bond separately in his tender, an appropriate item should be included in the Price List.

A sample form of performance bond is given in Appendix 5. This is based on
the ICE standard form of Default Bond which was drafted for use with the ICE
Conditions of Contract in collaboration with S. J. Berwin & Co.

Option X17: Low service damages

Low service damages **X17**

X17(1) If the Contractor produces substandard work the Employer can

- insist the Contractor corrects the Defect to provide the quality specified in the Service Information (clause 42.1),
- recover the cost of having it corrected by other people if the Contractor fails to correct the Defect within the specified time (clause 42.1) or
- accept the Defect and also a quotation from the Contractor for reduced Prices in return for a change to the Service Information (clause 43).

Where the performance of the service fails to reach the specified level due to a fault of the Contractor and the Defect is not or cannot be corrected, the Employer should be able to recover the damages he suffers in consequence. This Option provides for these damages to be recovered as liquidated damages. The required performance should be specified in the Service Information.

The low service damages included in the Contract Data in the service level table should be a genuine pre-estimate of the actual damages that the Employer will suffer as a result of the Contractor's breach. Under English law, damages greater than a genuine pre-estimate constitute a penalty and are not generally enforceable. The amount of damages are entered in the Contract Data part one against different ranges of low service.

Option X18: Limitation of liability

Limitation of liability **X18**

X18.1 to 18.3 Some situations under a TSC may involve risks of low probability but high impact. For this reason, it may be necessary for pure commercial reasons to limit the Contractor's liability for certain risks. These clauses state these limits, by reference to entries in the Contract Data.

X18.4 This clause seeks to state the Contractor's total liability, but with certain exclusions.

X18.5 This clause exempts the Contractor from any liability notified after the end of liability date which is stated in the Contract Data.

Option X19: Task Order

This Option can be used when all the services to be provided under the contract are to be instructed by Task Order, or when other services are being provided under the contract, and Tasks are added as necessary. For example the routine work may involve inspecting, cleaning and replacing lighting fittings to a highway when a light installation needs replacement, it would be ordered as a Task.

Providing the service **X19**

Identified and defined terms X19.1 A Task is limited to 'work within the service'. It is important therefore that the 'service' is drafted in the Contract Data sufficiently widely to include all work likely to be instructed by the Service Manager under the system of Task Orders.

The prices for the Task are added to the Price List.

X19.2   The specific work comprising a Task Order must have a starting date and a Task completion date. These dates are decided after consultation between the *Service Manager* and the *Contractor*. Obviously, in deciding these details it is essential to take into account the *Contractor*'s plan and resources. The amount of delay damages is also agreed. If these damages are determined unilaterally by the *Service Manager,* it is possible that they would not be enforceable if the matter was ever tested. For this reason alone, every attempt should be made to agree the details of the Task Order. A programme for each Task is also required to be prepared by the *Contractor* (clause X19.5 and X19.6).

When a Task Order is issued the priced list of items gets added to the Price List, thus increasing the total of the Prices. In addition the Service Information is changed to include this new item of work. That change is not a compensation event in itself, because the Price List has already been amended to take Into account the work in the Task Order.

Time   X19.4   The *Service Manager* can issue a Task Order up until the last day of the *service period*. This means that the Task Completion Date may be after the end of the *service period*. It is therefore necessary to extend the *service period* in this instance until the *Contractor* has completed the Task. This will ensure that the Parties' obligations concerning risks and insurances continue until all of the work is complete. However to ensure that the *service period* is not extended further no more Tasks can be issued during this extended period.

If the Task Completion Date is after the end of the *service period* that will also be a compensation event under clause X19.10(7). This enables the *Contractor* to recover any additional costs he may incur because he is carrying out this work in isolation after his main works have finished.

Task Order programme   X19.5   Since a Task is a discrete item of work, extending over a period of time, the *Contractor* is required to submit a programme to demonstrate how he proposes to carry out the Task. This permits proper monitoring and management of the Task. For small Tasks, the programme may be a simple one. For major and complex Tasks, the programme can assume considerable importance.

X19.6   This clause lists the information which the *Contractor* is required to show on each programme submitted for acceptance. It includes

- dates which are stated in the Task Order,
- dates decided by the *Contractor*,
- order and timing,
- float and, separately, time risk allowances,
- health and safety requirements and
- other information required in the Service Information.

The *Contractor*'s time risk allowances are to be shown on his programme as allowances attached to the duration of each activity or to the duration of parts of the Task. These allowances are owned by the *Contractor* as part of his realistic planning to cover his risks. They should be either clearly identified as such in the programme or included in the time periods allocated to specific activities. It follows that they should be retained in the assessment of any delay to planned Task Completion due to the effect of a compensation event.

Float is any spare time within the programme after the time risk allowances have been included. It is normally available to accommodate the time effects of a compensation event in order to mitigate or avoid any delay to planned Task Completion. Any delay to planned Task Completion due to a compensation event should be incorporated in a revised Programme showing details of the delay (see clause X19.11).

It is important that the time risk allowances included by the *Contractor* in a programme submitted for acceptance are realistic. If they are not, the *Service Manager* may refer to the first bullet point of clause X19.7 and refuse acceptance.

The provision for health and safety matters should allow for any statutory procedures, as well as those specifically mentioned in the Service Information.

The programme is also to show dates when the *Contractor* requires information, access, etc, which are to be provided to him by the *Employer*.

X19.7 This clause lists reasons why a *Service Manager* may decide not to accept a programme or a revised programme. Any failure by the *Service Manager* to accept a programme for reasons other than those noted is a compensation event (clause 60.1(8)). The *Service Manager* is required to respond within one week, but if there is non-acceptance, the *Contractor* is required to re submit within the *period for reply*.

Revising the Task Order programme

X19.8 This clause lists the matters which are to be shown on a revised Task Order programme. It should record the actual progress achieved on each operation and the reprogramming of future operations. It should also show the effects of implemented compensation events. If a compensation event affects the timing of future operations in Providing the Service, a revised plan indicating the effects is to be submitted as part of the *Contractor*'s quotation (clause 62.2). The revised programme should also show proposals for dealing with delays, Defects and any changes the *Contractor* wishes to make.

The *Service Manager* should note, in reviewing a submitted revised programme, any changes to the dates by which the *Employer* is required to provide information, facilities, access, etc. He should be prepared to accept a programme with earlier dates if this is acceptable to the *Employer*. After acceptance, any subsequent failure by the *Employer* to meet these earlier dates is a compensation event (clause X19.10(4)).

Compensation events

X19.10 The *Service Manager* has the authority to change a Task Order in the same way that he can change the Service Information. Such a change must result in a change to the Prices agreed for the Task Order. The change is assessed in the same way that other compensation events are assessed.

The second compensation event deals with a situation where the *Contractor* starts work in good faith (perhaps where the work is urgent) before he receives the Task Order. If, in such a case, the *Contractor* incurs costs which he would not otherwise have incurred if the Task Order had been issued before the starting date, those costs may well be reimbursed as a compensation event.

The fifth compensation event deals with failure by the *Employer* or Others to comply with the Task Order programme. This emphasises the need for the *Service Manager* to check carefully the relevant dates in any programme submitted by the *Contractor*.

The sixth compensation event is an event commonly described as 'force majeure'.

X19.11 This clause outlines the procedures for dealing with compensation events affecting a Task Order and their consequences. If a compensation event has the effect of delaying the *Contractor*'s activities in performing the Task, the *Contractor* is required to revise the programme and show the effects of any delay.

Option X20: Key Performance Indicators

X20.1 to X20.5 Key Performance Indicators (KPIs) are being increasingly used as a means of improving efficiency and encouraging better performance by contractors with a view to continuous improvement. KPIs are provided for in Option X12 where partnering arrangements are in place. This Option X20 can be used when Option X12 is not used. The procedure in Option X20 requires the establishment of performance targets and regular reporting by the *Contractor* of his performance measured against the KPIs.

OPTION Y

Option Y(UK)1: Project Bank Account

Y(UK)1   A secondary Option and associated Contract Data entries are provided for implementation of a Project Bank Account (PBA). The clause deals with payments into and out of the account, and its effect on other contract obligations.

Y1.1
(2)   Suppliers and Subcontractors at any level, known as "Named Suppliers", can be included in the PBA arrangements. The *Contractor* will initially identify those to be included at tender (*named suppliers*), but subject to the acceptance of the *Service Manager*, the *Contractor* can add further Suppliers during the contract.

The *Employer* should set out in the Service Information any stipulations or restrictions on establishing the list of suppliers who can participate in payments from the PBA.

If Option Y(UK)3 is used, the rights of Named Suppliers need to be listed in the Contract Data.

Y1.1
(5)
and (6)   The forms to be used for the Trust Deed and the Joinging Deed are included in the TSC. These forms must be included in the contract, placed after the entry in the Contract Data for Y1.1.

Y1.2,
1.3   The PBA is established and maintained by the *Contractor*, who pays any bank charges and retains any interest earned on the account, unless the *Employer* states in the Contract Data that these will be paid and received by the *Employer*. At tender, the *Contractor* must identify a suitable bank able to offer arrangements which comply with the requirements for payment in this Option.

Y1.4   The banking arrangements must make provision for payments to be made in accordance with the contract. This must be, at the latest, the date for payment set out in clause 51.2, and must take account of the times for submission of the Authorisation and the timing of payments into the account.

Y1.5   Contract arrangements with Named Suppliers must include the relevant parts of this Option in the subcontract. Guidance on how to prepare the appropriate provisions is given in the section of these guidance notes on subcontracting.

Y1.7   The *Contractor* is required to submit an application for payment, showing the amounts due to each Named Supplier, following which the *Service Manager* issues a certificate as normal.

Y1.8   The *Employer* pays to the PBA the amount certified, subject to any withheld sums notified to the *Contractor*. If the *Employer* withholds payment from the *Contractor* which results in the *Contractor*'s payment being negative, the *Contractor* is required to pay into to the account any amount needed to make payment in full to Named Suppliers.

Y1.9   The *Contractor* prepares the Authorisation, confirming the payments to Named Suppliers, and forwards it to the *Project Manager* for the *Employer*'s counter-signature. The Authorisation is for the amount of payment to be made by the *Employer*; that is the certified amount less any notified withholding. The Authorisation is then forwarded to the bank – it is envisaged that electronic means of authorisation will be used to simplify this process. The *Employer* should not attempt to establish whether payments to Named Suppliers has been calculated correctly – that it the *Contractor*'s responsibility.

Y1.10   The *project bank* makes payment to the *Contractor* and Named Suppliers from the sums deposited.

Y1.13 The Trust Deed is intended to allow payment to Named Suppliers to continue in the event of the insolvency of the *Contractor*. The deed is executed by the *Employer*, *Contractor* and initial *named suppliers*.

Where an additional Supplier is to be joined into the deed, a Joining Deed needs to be executed by the *Employer*, *Contractor* and the Additional Supplier. A copy of the initial Trust Deed should be annexed to each Joining Deed.

The payment arrangements, and how these fit with other contract provisions, are shown in the following chart.

Timescales for assessment and payment under Project Bank Account arrangements

Clause 51 dates	Clause 51 actions	Project Bank Account actions	Y(UK)2 actions	Y(UK)2 dates
assessment date	*Contractor* may submit application for payment	*Contractor* submits application for payment showing amounts due to Named Suppliers		
assessment date + 1 week	*Service Manager* assesses amount due and certifies payment		date on which payment becomes due	assessment date + 7 days
			Latest date for notifying intention to pay less	assessment date + 14 days
		Contractor prepares and signs Authorisation, forwards to *Service Manager*. *Contractor* makes payment to Project Bank Account of any amount withheld by *Employer*		
		Employer signs Authorisation, issues to project bank and makes payment to Project Bank Account		
assessment date + 3 weeks	*Employer* or *Contractor* makes certified payment	Payment made to *Contractor* and Named Suppliers from Project Bank Account	Final date for payment	assessment date + 21 days

Note: Y(UK)2 seven day periods could be longer than clause 51 week periods, as former excludes Christmas Day, Good Friday and bank holidays from count of days.

Option Y(UK)2: The Housing Grants, Construction and Regeneration Act 1996

Y(UK)2

Y2.1   In the NEC family of contracts periods of time are usually measured in weeks thus avoiding complications of rest days and statutory holidays in different countries in which these contracts are used. The UK Housing Grants, Construction and Regeneration Act 1996 as amended by the Local Democracy, Economic Development and Construction Act 2009 (the Act), however, defines most periods as a number of days. Section 116(3) of the Act states that Christmas Day, Good Friday and bank holidays are excluded from any period specified in the Act. Where the time period associated with the Act is referred to, that period has been stated in days in Option Y(UK)2.

   The key periods affecting the procedure for payments when Option Y(UK)2 applies are illustrated in Figure 1, which includes references to the Act and to the Y(UK)2 clauses. Figure 1 should be referred to in conjunction with the following notes on clauses Y2.2 to Y2.4.

Y2.2   In order to comply with Section 110 of the Act, this clause defines when the payment becomes due and the final date for payment. It also confirms that the *Service Manager*'s certificate, issued in accordance with core clause 51.1 is the notice of payment required by Section 110A of the Act. This certificate is required to show the basis upon which the payment has been calculated.

Y2.3   In order to comply with Section 111 of the Act this clause sets out the requirement that, if the paying Party wishes to pay less than the sum set out in the *Service Manager*'s certificate, they must give a notice setting out the amount they intend to pay and the basis upon which it has been calculated. This notice must be given at least 7 days before the final date for payment set out in Y2.2. Without such notice the paying Party is required to pay the sum in the *Service Manager*'s certificate.

Y2.4   Under Section 112 of the Act the *Contractor* has the right to suspend performance of all or any part of the *service* if

- he is not paid the amount set out in the *Service Manager*'s certificate by the final date for payment, unless a notice to pay a lesser sum has been given in accordance with Y2.3, or
- if a notice to pay a lesser sum has been given in accordance with Y2.3, and that lesser sum has not been paid by the final date for payment.

   If the *Contractor* exercises this right it is a compensation event.

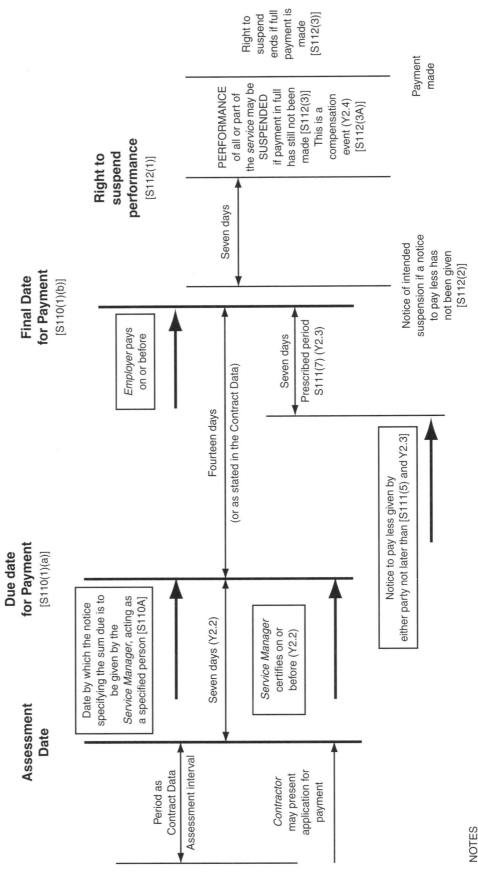

Figure 1. Construction Act – Payment Periods

NOTES
1. Durations stated in days include weekends but exclude Christmas Day, Good Friday and bank holidays. [S116]

Option Y(UK)3: The Contracts (Rights of Third Parties) Act 1999

Y(UK)3

Y3.1   If it is decided to give rights under the contract to a third party, it is important that the rights are clearly stated in the Contract Data by reference to clauses in the *conditions of contract*.

Option Z: *Additional conditions of contract*

This Option should be used where the *Employer* wishes to include additional conditions. These should be carefully drafted in the same style as the core and optional clauses, using the same defined terms and other terminology. They should be carefully checked for consistency with the other conditions.

Additional conditions should be used only where absolutely necessary to accommodate special needs. The flexibility of the TSC main and secondary Options minimises the need for additional conditions. Additional conditions should never be used for matters which should properly be included in the Service Information, e.g. constraints on how the *Contractor* is to Provide the Service. The important difference is that the Service Information can be varied by the *Service Manager* under clause 14.3 whereas information in the *conditions of contract* cannot be changed under the contract.

APPENDIX 1

Clause numbering system

1 General

Core			Options			
Cl. no.	Title	Subcl. no.	Cl. no.	Title	Subcl. no.	Applicable options
10	Actions	10.1				
11	Identified and defined terms	11.1 11.2(1) to (16)				
				PSPD	11.2(17)	A
				PSPD	11.2(18)	C
				PSPD	11.2(18)	E
				Prices	11.2(19)	A
				Prices	11.2(20)	C
12	Interpretation and the law	12.1 to 12.4		Prices	11.2(21)	E
13	Communications	13.1 to 13.8				
14	The *Service Manager*	14.1 to 14.4				
15	Employer provides right of access and things	15.1 15.2				
16	Early warning	16.1 to 16.4				
17	Ambiguities and inconsistencies	17.1				
18	Illegal and impossible requirements	18.1				

2 The *Contractor*'s main responsibilities

Core			Options			
Cl. no.	Title	Subcl. no.	Cl. no.	Title	Subcl. no.	Applicable Options
20	Providing the Service	20.1 20.2				
					20.3 to 20.4 20.5	C, E A
21	The *Contractor*'s plan	21.1 to 21.3				
					21.4	A, C
22	Revising the *Contractor*'s plan	22.1				
23	Design of Equipment	23.1				
24	People	24.1 24.2				
25	Working with the *Employer* and Others	25.1 25.2				
26	Subcontracting	26.1 to 26.3			26.4	C, E
27	Other responsibilities	27.1 to 27.4				

3 Time

Core			Options			
Cl. no.	Title	Subcl. no.	Cl. no.	Title	Subcl. no.	Applicable Options
30	Starting and the *service period*	30.1				
31	Access	31.1				
32	Instructions to stop or not to start work	32.1				

4 Testing and Defects

Core			Options			
Cl. no.	Title	Subcl. no.	Cl. no.	Title	Subcl. no.	Applicable Options
40	Tests and inspections	40.1 to 40.6				
41	Testing and inspection before delivery	41.1				
42	Notifying and correcting Defects	42.1 to 42.3				
43	Accepting Defects	43.1				

5 Payment

Core			Options			
Cl. no.	Title	Subcl. no.	Cl. no.	Title	Subcl. no.	Applicable Options
50	Assessing the amount due	50.1 to 50.5			50.6 50.7	C E
51	Payment	51.1 to 51.4				
52	Defined Cost	52.1			52.2 52.3	C, E C, E
			53	The *Contractor*'s share	53.1 to 53.3	C
			54	The Price List	54.1 to 54.3	A, C

6 Compensation events

Core			Options			
Cl. no.	Title	Subcl. no.	Cl. no.	Title	Subcl. no.	Applicable Options
60	Compensation events	60.1(1) to (14)				
61	Notifying compensation events	61.1 to 61.7				
62	Quotations for compensation events	62.1 to 62.6				
63	Assessing compensation events	63.1 to 63.9			63.10 63.11 63.12 63.13	A C A, C A
64	The *Service Manager*'s assessments	64.1 to 64.3				
65	Implementing compensation events	65.1 65.2				
					65.3 65.4	A, C E

7 Use of equipment, Plant and Materials

Core			Options			
Cl. no.	Title	Subcl. no.	Cl. no.	Title	Subcl. no.	Applicable Options
70	The Parties' use of equipment, Plant and Materials	70.1 70.2				

8 Risks and insurance

Core			Options			
Cl. no.	Title	Subcl. no.	Cl. no.	Title	Subcl. no.	Applicable Options
80	*Employer*'s risks	80.1				
81	The *Contractor*'s risks	81.1				
82	Indemnity	82.1 82.2				
83	Insurance cover	83.1 83.2				
84	Insurance policies	84.1 to 84.4				
85	If the *Contractor* does not insure	85.1				
86	Insurance by the *Employer*	86.1 to 86.3				

9 Termination

Core			Options			
Cl. no.	Title	Subcl. no.	Cl. no.	Title	Subcl. no.	Applicable Options
90	Termination	90.1 to 90.5				
91	Reasons for termination	91.1 to 91.7				
92	Procedures on termination	92.1 92.2				
93	Payment on termination	93.1 93.2				
					93.3 93.4	C C

Dispute resolution

OPTION W1		OPTION W2	
Clause	Title	Clause	Title
W1.1	Dispute resolution	W2.1	Dispute resolution
W1.2	The *Adjudicator*	W2.2	The *Adjudicator*
W1.3	The adjudication	W2.3	The adjudication
W1.4	Review by the *tribunal*	W2.4	Review by the *tribunal*

Secondary Option clauses

Clause no.	Secondary Option	Clause title	Clause no.

X1	Price adjustment for inflation (used only with Options A and C)	Defined terms
		Price Adjustment Factor
		Compensation events
		Price adjustment
		   Option A
		   Option C
			X1.1
			X1.2
			X1.3
			
			X1.4
			X1.5

X2	Changes in the law	Changes in the law	X2.1
X3	Multiple currencies (used only with Option A)	Multiple currencies	X3.1 X3.2
X4	Parent company guarantee	Parent company guarantee	X4.1
X12	Partnering	Identified and defined terms Actions Working together Incentives	X12.1(1) to (5) X12.2(1) to (6) X12.3(1) to (9) X12.4(1) & (2)
X13	Performance bond	Performance bond	X13.1
X17	Low service damages	Low service damages	X17.1
X18	Limitation of liability	Limitation of liability	X18.1 to X18.5
X19	Task Order	Defined terms Providing the *service* Time Task Order programme Revising the Task Order programme Compensation events Implementing compensation events	X19.1(1) to (4) X19.2 X19.3 X19.4 X19.5 to X19.7 X19.8 to X19.9 X19.10 X19.11 X19.12
X20	Key Performance Indicators	Incentives	X20.1 to X20.5
Y(UK)1	Project Bank Account		Y1.1 to Y1.14
Y(UK)2	The Housing Grants, Construction and Regeneration Act 1996	Definitions Dates for payment Notice of intention to pay less Suspension of performance	Y2.1 Y2.2 Y2.3 Y2.4
Y(UK)3	The Contracts (Rights of Third Parties) Act 1999	Third party rights	Y3.1
Z	*Additional conditions of contract*	*Additional conditions of contract*	Z1.1

APPENDIX 2

Sample form of tender

TENDER

The *service* . . . .

To. . . . .(the *Employer*)

Address . . . .

. . . .

. . . .

. . . .

We offer to Provide the Service in accordance with the Contract Data part one and the attached Contract Data part two for a sum to be determined in accordance with the *conditions of contract.*

You may accept this offer on or before [date of last day for acceptance]

Yours faithfully,

Signed. . . . .

Name. . . . .

Position . . . .

On behalf of. . . . .(the *Contractor*)

Address . . . .

. . . .

. . . .

. . . .

Date. . . . .

APPENDIX 3

Sample form of agreement

This agreement is made on the . . . . day of . . . . 20. . . . between

- . . . .

    of . . . .

    . . . . (the *Employer*) and

- . . . .

    of . . . .

    . . . . (the *Contractor*)

The *Employer* wishes to have the following *service* provided:

. . . .

. . . .

. . . .

1 The *Contractor* will Provide the Service in accordance with the *conditions* of *contract* identified in the Contract Data.

2 The *Employer* will pay the *Contractor* the amount due and carry out his duties in accordance with the *conditions of contract* identified in the Contract Data.

3 The documents forming part of this agreement are:

- the *Contractor*'s tender
- the *Employer*'s letter of acceptance
- the Price List
- the Contract Data part one
- the Contract Data part two
- the following documents

. . . .

. . . .

. . . .

. . . .

. . . .

Signed by

Name. . . . .

Position . . . .

On behalf of (*Employer*) . . . .

and

Name. . . . .

Position . . . .

On behalf of (*Contractor*) . . . .

ALTERNATIVE IF AGREEMENT IF EXECUTED AS A DEED

EXECUTED AS A DEED BY THE *EMPLOYER* (where the *Employer* is a company)

. . . .(name of Director)

. . . .(signature of Director)

. . . .(name of Director or Company Secretary)

. . . . (signature of Director or Company Secretary)

AND AS A DEED BY THE *CONTRACTOR* (where the *Contractor* is a company)

. . . .(name of Director)

. . . .(signature of Director)

. . . .(name of Director or Company Secretary)

. . . . (signature of Director or Company Secretary)

APPENDIX 4

Use of the TSC as a subcontract

The TSC can be used as a subcontract. If so, it will need to be adapted as suggested in the following notes, which should be read in conjunction with the main guidance notes

Options

Use of the TSC as a subcontract ensures as far as possible that the two contracts are 'back-to-back'. This minimises the risk to the *Contractor* as he passes his risks to the Subcontractor in respect of the work in the subcontract. However, it is possible that the *Contractor* may select a main Option for the subcontract which is different from the main Option in the main contract. For example, the main contract may be carried out under Option C, but it may be more appropriate to carry out the subcontract under Option A. This will affect such things as payment and assessment of compensation events (see below).

Identification of terms

The *Employer* named in the Contract Data for the subcontract would be the Contractor (X) in the main contract. The *Contractor* named in the subcontract would be the Subcontractor (Y) in the subcontract. The parties to the subcontract would then be main Contractor (X) and Subcontractor (Y), replacing the *Employer* and *Contractor* respectively.

It facilitates management of the subcontract if a person equivalent to the *Service Manager* in the main contract is appointed in the subcontract. It is recommended that he is described as the '*Contractor*'s *Service Manager*' in the subcontract.

To avoid confusion, in these notes, the terms Employer, Contractor, Subcontractor, Service Manager and Contractor's Service Manager (without italics) are used.

TSC main contract	*Employer*	*Contractor*		*Service Manager*
TSC as subcontract		*Employer*	*Contractor*	*Contractor*'s *Service Manager*
Terms used in this guidance note	Employer	Contractor (X)	Subcontractor (Y)	Service Manager

The *Adjudicator* in the subcontract should be appointed in the same way as in the main contract

Service Information

The Contractor should prepare the Service Information for the subcontract thoroughly to ensure that the subcontracted work is properly undertaken by the Subcontractor in accordance with the requirements of the main contract.

The following information about the main contract should be included in the subcontract.

- Title of the main contract Service.
- Name of the main contract Employer.
- Name of the main contract Service Manager.

Subcontractor's plan	The Contractor should ensure that the information (dates, methods, timing, procedures, etc.) which he requires to be shown on the Subcontractor's plan is consistent with, and is such as to enable him to comply with, his own Plan and other obligations in the main contract. These requirements should be included in the Subcontract Service Information.
Payment	In the main contract, Defined Cost includes payments for 'subcontracted work'. If the main contract is under Option C, the Price for Services Provided to Date (PSPD) is in terms of the Defined Cost which the Contractor has paid. Thus, before the main Contractor can include payment for subcontracted work in his monthly invoice, he must already have paid the Subcontractor. The subcontract may well be under Option A, in which case the amount paid to the Subcontractor (PSPD) is for the work in the Subcontract Price List which the Subcontractor has carried out.
Compensation events	In order to allow adequate time for the involvement of a Subcontractor in the assessment of a compensation event which affects the main contract, careful consideration should be given to adjustment of the time periods. The following additional conditions of contract, which are suggested as a guide, should be entered in the Contract Data for the Subcontract.

'In these conditions of contract the periods of time in the clauses stated are changed as follows:

- Clause 61.3, second sentence, 'eight weeks' is changed to 'seven weeks'.
- Clause 61.4, fifth bullet, 'one week' is changed to 'two weeks'.
- Clause 61.4, last sentence, 'two weeks' is changed to 'three weeks'.
- Clause 62.3, first sentence, 'three weeks' is changed to 'one week'.
- Clause 62.3, second sentence, 'two weeks' is changed to 'four weeks'.
- Clause 62.6, third sentence, 'two weeks' is changed to 'three weeks'.
- Clause 64.3, fifth sentence, 'two weeks' is changed to 'three weeks'.

Disputes	A provision should be included to cater for a dispute arising under the main contract which concerns the subcontract. This enables the Contractor to require that such a dispute can be dealt with jointly with the dispute under the main contract by the main contract *Adjudicator*. This avoids two different adjudicators making different decisions on the same dispute.

The subcontract *Adjudicator* may be a person different from the main contract *Adjudicator*. His function is to deal with disputes which arise only between the Contractor and Subcontractor and which do not concern the Employer.

If any of the three parties to a joint dispute disagrees with the *Adjudicator*'s decision, he may refer it to the *tribunal*, as in the case of a dispute between only two contracting parties.

Insurance	By providing part of the *service* as a subcontract, the Contractor in effect, passes to the Subcontractor those of the Contractor's risks under the main contract which apply to work in the subcontract. Double insurance is largely avoided since the insurance premiums payable by the Contractor under the main contract will reflect the proportion of the services which are subcontracted.

Project bank account

The clauses for Option Y(UK)1 should be modified in the subcontract. The following changes should be made.

'Named Supplier' should become 'Subcontract Named Supplier'.

Clauses 1.2 to 1.4 and 1.8 should be deleted and subsequent clauses renumbered.

Additional clause shall be added.

'The *Contractor* and his employer make payment into the *project bank* of the amount stated in the Authorisation'.

Depending on whether the Subcontractor is identified as a *named supplier* in the Contract Data for the *Contractor*'s contract with his employer, include provisions for signing the Trust Deed or Joining Deed as appropriate.

In the Contract Data entries, omit the entry for payment of charges and interest of the *project bank*, and the entry identifying the *project bank*.

APPENDIX 5

TSC Form of Performance Bond

Date

Parties

[Names and addresses and company numbers if applicable]

SURETY (1)

CONTRACTOR (2)

EMPLOYER (3)

Background

(A) By a Contract defined in the Schedule hereto the Contractor has agreed with the Employer to Provide the Service.

(B) The Surety has agreed to provide this Bond in favour of the Employer in order to guarantee the performance by the Contractor of his obligations under the Contract.

Surety's obligation   1

(1) If the Contractor fails to pay the Excess Sum within 28 days of receipt by the Contractor of the payment certificate under clause 90.4 of the Contract the Surety hereby guarantees to the Employer that the Surety shall subject to the terms and conditions of this Bond pay the Excess Sum in accordance with clause 1(3) up to the Bond Amount.

(2) It shall be a condition precedent to payment by the Surety that the Employer send to the Surety a copy of any notification and certificate under clause 90.1 of the Contract and of any certificate issued under clause 90.4 of the Contract within 14 days of such notification or certificate being served on the Contractor and that any copy certificate sent to the Surety shall be certified by the Service Manager as being a true copy of his certificate.

(3) Subject to clause 1(4) payment by the Surety shall be made not later than 28 days after the later of

(a) the expiry of the 28 day period referred to in clause 1(1) (save in respect of any payment made by the Contractor within that time) and

(b) service on the Surety of the copy certificate referred to in clause 1(2).

(4) If the Surety objects to the contents of or entitlement to issue a certificate under clause 90.4 of the Contract in respect of which the Employer seeks payment from him the Surety shall have the right to refer the matter to adjudication in accordance with the adjudication provisions contained in Option W1 or W2 whichever is applicable, of the Contract as if the Surety were a party to the Contract in place of the Contractor.

(5) Any adjudication under clause 1(4) shall be commenced by the Surety within 14 days of receipt by the Surety of the documents referred to in clause 1(2) and the Surety shall have no right to refer the matter to adjudication after that time.

                                                                                          www.neccontract.com

(6) If the content of or entitlement to issue the certificate under clause 90.4 of the Contract in respect of which payment is sought by the Employer is or has been prior to the occurrence in relation to the Contractor of any of the events set out at clause 91.1 of the Contract the subject of an adjudicator's decision in an adjudication between the Employer and Contractor under the Contract the Surety agrees to be bound by the result of such adjudication and shall have no right to refer the matter to adjudication under clause 1(4).

(7) In the case of an adjudication under clause 1(4) payment by the Surety shall be made within 7 days of the decision in such adjudication.

Surety's rights 2

(1) The Employer shall send to the Surety copies of any notification or certificate given by the Service Manager under clause 90.1 of the Contract and any certificate issued under clause 90.4 in each case within 14 days of such notification or certificate being served on the Contractor.

(2) The Surety shall be entitled at any time within 7 days of receipt by the Surety of the copy certificate referred to in clause 1(2)

(a) to require the Employer to provide the Surety with such further information and documentation as the Surety may reasonably require to verify the Excess Sum (including information and documentation held by the Service Manager) and/or

(b) to request to inspect the Affected Property upon reasonable notice (the Employer may require that a representative of the Employer accompanies the Surety during such inspections).

Accounting 3

(1) If the Excess Sum is subsequently determined by reason of a subsequent certificate issued by the Service Manager under clause 51.1 or by adjudication arbitration litigation or agreement between the Surety and the Employer to be less than the amount paid by the Surety the difference (if the Excess Sum has already been paid by the Surety) shall be repaid by the Employer to the Surety with Interest within 14 days (or such other period as the adjudicator arbitrator or Court may direct) after the date of such determination or agreement.

(2) If the Excess Sum is subsequently determined or agreed to be greater than the amount already paid by the Surety any difference (up to the Bond Amount) shall be paid by the Surety to the Employer within 14 days (or such other period as the adjudicator arbitrator or Court may direct) after the date of such determination or agreement.

Interest 4

Subject to the amount payable by the Surety being varied in accordance with clause 3 above in the event that any amount payable by either the Surety or the Employer under this bond is not made by the date determined by clause 1(3) or in accordance with clause 3 (the Due Date) then the payer shall pay Interest on the sum from whichever shall be the earlier of the Due Date and the date

Expiry 5

Save in respect of any failure to pay the Excess Sum in respect of which a claim in writing has been received beforehand from the Employer by the Surety this Bond shall expire on the later of the end of the service period stated in the Contract and the Final Expiry Date.

Forbearance 6

The Surety shall not be discharged or released by any alteration variation or waiver of any of the terms and conditions and provisions of the Contract or in any extent or nature of the Service and no allowance of time by the Employer under or in connection with the Contract or the Service shall in any way release reduce or affect the liability of the Surety under this Bond.

Governing law 7

This Bond shall be governed and construed in accordance with the law of the contract stated in the Contract and the courts administering such law shall have exclusive jurisdiction.

Assignment 8   This Bond may only be assigned by the Employer with the prior consent of the Surety and the Contractor which consent shall not be unreasonably withheld. In the event of any such assignment the Employer and assignee shall remain jointly and severally liable for any repayment due to the Surety under clause 3(1). Notice of any assignment shall be given to the Surety as soon as practicable.

Third Parties 9   Nothing in this Bond confers or purports to confer on any third party any benefit or any right pursuant to the Contracts (Rights of Third Parties) Act 1999 to enforce any term of this Bond.

EXECUTED AS A DEED

on behalf of the Surety   (1)   director . . . .

     (2)   director/secretary . . . .

on behalf of the Contractor   (1)   director . . . .

     (2)   director/secretary . . . .

on behalf of the Employer   (1)   director . . . .

     (2)   director/secretary . . . .

SCHEDULE

Address for Service   **Contractor:**

Tel: Fax:

Employer:

Tel: Fax:

Surety:

Tel: Fax:

'Bond Amount'   means the sum of £[   ] ([   ] pounds) being the maximum aggregate liability of the Surety under this Bond.

'Contract'   means the contract [made between the Employer and the Contractor dated the [   ] day of [   ] [   ]/[to be entered into between the Employer and the Contractor] incorporating the NEC Term Service Contract 1st Edition.

'Excess Sum'   an amount as certified as due under clause 90.4 of the Contract.

'Service Manager' 'Service' and 'Affected Property'   have the same meaning as in the Contract.

'Final Expiry Date'   means the [   ] day of [   ] [   ].

'Interest'   means the rate of interest specified in the Contract.

(This Bond is based on the ICE Form of Default Bond dated May 2003 which was issued for use with the ICE Conditions of Contract. The ICE Default Bond was drafted in collaboration with S. J. BERWIN & Co)

APPENDIX 6

Price List

Entries in the first four columns in this Price List are made either by the *Employer* or the tendering contractor. For Option E the Price List is used only for forecasting Defined Cost.

If the *Contractor* is to be paid an amount for the item which is not adjusted if the quantity of work in the item changes, the tendering contractor enters the amount in the Price column only, the Unit, Expected Quantity and Rate columns being left blank.

If the *Contractor* is to be paid an amount for the item of work which is the rate for the work multiplied by the quantity completed, the tendering contractor enters the rate which is then multiplied by the Expected Quantity to produce the Price, which is also entered.

If the *Contractor* is to be paid a Price for an item proportional to the length of time for which a service is provided, a unit of time is stated in the Unit column and the expected length of time (as a quantity of the stated units of time) is stated in the Expected Quantity column.

Item nr	Description	Unit	Expected Quantity	Rate	Price

The total of the Prices ☐

APPENDIX 7

Contract Data – worked example

Introduction

The following pages show the Contract Data completed for a fictitious contract. The purpose of this example is to help those unfamiliar with the NEC system to complete the tender documents. It should be read in conjunction with the notes included under in Chapter 4.

The following points should be noted.

- The TSC text of the Contract Data formats is reproduced as printed, together with the explanatory sentences which are in bold type. The explanatory sentences (e.g. 'Statements given in all contracts' and sentences beginning 'If...') are only for the guidance of users and should not be reproduced on an actual Contract Data.

- For clarity, quantities have been inserted in the appropriate places. **The figures given are imaginary and should not be taken as typical and certainly do not have the status of 'recommended by the NEC Panel'.** The examples of entries are not necessarily consistent throughout.

- Most optional statements have been completed so that users can see what should be written if that Option is chosen. **In a real enquiry only those statements relevant to the Options chosen should be completed.**

- If an optional statement is required it should be inserted in an appropriate position in the actual Contract Data, within the statements for the relevant section of the TSC.

- **The statements in the boxes only provide a very abbreviated commentary on completing the Contract Data and should not be relied on.** Reference must be made to the conditions themselves and to the relevant guidance notes for a fuller treatment of topics.

- **The *Employer* must decide actual details based on the nature of the contract and the allocation of risk required.**

- **Those drawing up tender documents are advised to take care when completing the Contract Data that excessive risks are not passed to the *Contractor*.** The TSC system is much more flexible than any other published contract and allows a wide range of *Employer*'s choice of allocation of risks on the *Contractor*, which would be limited in other documents. **Common sense needs to be applied otherwise bids will reflect the unrealistic aspirations of the *Employer*.** In particular combinations including large bonds, fixed prices and heavy low service damages should only be used if the *Employer*'s key strategy demands them.

- **The words of the TSC Contract Data formats should be reproduced without change.** Users of the TSC are granted a limited licence by the Institution of Civil Engineers to reproduce the text in tenders solely for the purpose of inviting, assessing and managing contracts.

Part one – Data provided by the *Employer*

Completion of the data in full, according to the Options chosen, is essential to create a complete contract.

Statements given in all contracts

1 General

- The *conditions of contract* are the core clauses and the clauses for main Option A, dispute resolution Option **W1** and secondary Options **X2, X17, X18, X19, X20, and Z** of the NEC3 Term Service Contract April 2013.

Note that this statement is not included if Y(NZ)1 used.

Choose one main Option (A to F) and one main Option (W1 or W2) unless Y(NZ)1 is used. In addition choose any of the secondary Options appropriate to the chosen contract strategy, ensuring that these are compatible with the chosen main Option. This might include Y(NZ)1 or Y(NZ)2 if these Options were correctly to be included, in this example they are not incorporated.

- The *service* is **providing facilities management services to the head office of More Sustainability Ltd in Christchurch, New Zealand.**

Describe the *service* clearly but briefly. The description should enable the *service* to be identified but should not go into details; details will be included in the Service Information. It may be helpful to include the location of the *service* if this is not clear from the description.

It is sensible to use a shorter title in correspondence – in this case 'More Sustainability – FM services' would be an obvious choice.

The *Employer*'s legal name and usual address are given here. The address need not be the registered office unless the applicable law so requires.

- The *Employer* is

Name **More Sustainability Ltd.**

Address **Eco Road**
Christchurch
New Zealand
Tel + 64 (03-333 3333).

It is essential that the person chosen as *Service Manager* is sufficiently close to the work and have the time to carry out his duties effectively. He must also have sufficient authority to exercise the authority given to him under the contract.

See the guidance notes (GNs) on the *Service Manager*.

- The *Service Manager* is

Name **Mrs I Certifier**

Address **I C Consultants**
Bridge Road
Christchurch
New Zealand.

Note that this statement is not included if Y(NZ)1 used.

- The *Adjudicator* is

Name ....

Address ....
....
....
....

The *Adjudicator* proposed by the *Employer* can be named here, a list of suggested names could be proposed, here or in the Instructions to Tenderers, or the provisions can be left blank. If the latter, W1 and W2 provide a process for determining the *Adjudicator* post contract, if indeed a dispute arises.

- The Affected Property is **the head office of More Sustainability Ltd in Christchurch, New Zealand, including the car parking and adjacent landscaping areas**

See GNs on clause 11.2(2).

State references of the documents containing the Service Information.

- The Service Information is in **document ref FM/Gen1.**

- The *language of this contract* is **English.**

It is possible for the law of one country to be applied in the courts of another. Thus the place of jurisdiction should be stated here as well as the law that is to apply to the contract.

- The *law of the contract* is the law of **New Zealand.**

- The *period for reply* is **two weeks.**

The *period for reply* (see GNs on clause 13.3) must be sufficient for the parties to respond, but should be sufficiently brief to maintain the principle of dealing with problems before they arise.

- The *Adjudicator nominating body* is the **Building Disputes Tribunal NZ Ltd.**

Care should be taken when choosing the *Adjudicator* – see notes on Dispute Resolution options for their relevant experience, qualifications and ability.

The Institution of Civil Engineers maintains a list of suitably qualified and experienced people to act as adjudicators. Several other institutions maintain similar lists.

The choice is usually between arbitration and litigation

- The *tribunal* is **litigation.**

- The following matters will be included in the Risk Register
  Possible change of access security requirements during 2014
  Limited car parking availability for *Contractor*'s **personnel**
  On-going lift replacement contract due to end December 2014
  On-site cafeteria to be separately refurbished during 2013
  Possible increase of *Employer*'s **staff numbers by 20% during 2014**
  Small extension to property commencing 2014.

The *Employer* lists here the risks that he requires to be included in the Risk Register. This alerts the tenderer to the risks, and encourages the *Service Manager* and the *Contractor* to discuss how best to avoid or minimise their effects.

3 Time
- The *starting date* is **1 May 2013.**

See GNs on clause 30.1.

- The *service period* is **two years.**

See GNs on clause 30.1.

5 Payment
- The *assessment interval* is **monthy**

The limit of five weeks is to ensure a reasonable cash flow for the *Contractor*. In practice most payment procedures will be based on calendar months.

- The *currency of this contract* is the **New Zealand dollar.**

The *Employer* should select a bank to reflect the *currency of this contract*, not necessarily the country where the *service* are being carried out.

- The *interest rate* is **4** % per annum (not less than 2) above the **base lending** rate of the **Reserve Bank of New Zealand.**

8 Risks and insurance
- The minimum amount of cover for insurance against loss of or damage caused by the *Contractor* to the *Employer*'s property is **$1,000,000 (one million dollars).**

- The minimum amount of cover for insurance in respect of loss of or damage to property (except the *Employer*'s property, Plant and Materials and Equipment) and liability for bodily injury to or death of a person (not an employee of the *Contractor*) arising from or in connection with the *Contractor*'s Providing the Service for any one event is **$10,000,000 (ten million dollars).**

Unless the *Employer* has his own insurance department or access to insurance specialists, it is sensible to get advice on the figures to be inserted here.

This will be especially true when working outside the UK.

- The minimum limit of indemnity for insurance in respect of death of or bodily injury to employees of the *Contractor* arising out of and in the course of their employment in connection with this contract for any one event is **$10,000,000 (ten million dollars).**

Optional statements

If the *tribunal* is arbitration

See GN on clause W1.4 or W2.4.

- The *arbitration procedure* is **the latest version of the Institution of Civil Engineers Arbitration Procedure in force when the arbitrator is appointed.**
- The place where arbitration is to be held is **Auckland.**
- The person or organisation who will choose an arbitrator
  - if the Parties cannot agree a choice or
  - if the *arbitration procedure* does not state who selects an arbitrator is
  The Institution of Civil Engineers of the United Kingdom.

If no plan is identified in part two of the Contract Data

See GNs on clause 21.1.

- The *Contractor* submits a first plan for acceptance within **two** weeks of the Contract Date.

If the period in which payments are made is not three weeks and Y(NZ)1 is not used

- The period within which payments are made is **one** week.

Include this provision if Y(NZ)1 is not incorporated, and the 3 weeks default payment period in clause 51.2 is to be changed. If Y(NZ)1 is used then see the guidance on that secondary Option.

See GNs on clause 51.1.

If Y(UK)2 is used and the final date for payment is not 14 days after the date when payment is due

- The period for payment is..

This provision would be added in were Y(NZ)1 incorporated.

If Y(UK)2 is used and the Due Date for Payment is not 17 days after the assessment date

- **The Due Date for Payment is .... days after the assessment date.**

If there are additional *Employer*'s risks

- These are additional *Employer*'s risks

  1 ....

  2 ....

  3 ....

It may not be economical for the *Contractor* to assume a particular risk, especially a risk that has a low probability of occurrence but a very serious consequence.

Insert the value or replacement cost of any 'free issue' Plant or Materials to be incorporated in the *service*.

If the *Employer* is to provide Plant and Materials

- The insurance against loss of or damage to Plant and Materials is to include cover for Plant and Materials provided by the *Employer* for an amount of **$50,000 (fifty thousand dollars).**

If the *Employer* is to provide any of the insurances stated in the Insurance Table

- The *Employer* provides these insurances from the Insurance Table

  1 Insurance against ....

  Cover/indemnity is ....

  The deductibles are ....

  2 Insurance against ....

  Cover/indemnity is ....

  The deductibles are ....

  3 Insurance against ....

  Cover/indemnity is ....

  The deductibles are ....

If the *Employer* has decided to provide any of the insurances, details should be entered here.

See GNs on clause 86.1.

State any additional insurances to be provided by the *Employer*. This may include special arrangements.

See GNs on Section 8.

If additional insurances are to be provided

- The *Employer* provides these additional insurances

  1 Insurance against...

  Cover/indemnity is...

  The deductibles are ....

  2 Insurance against...

  Cover/indemnity is...

  The deductibles are ....

- The *Contractor* provides these additional insurances

  1 Insurance against...

  Cover/indemnity is...

  The deductibles are ....

  2 Insurance against...

  Cover/indemnity is...

  The deductibles are ....

If Option A is used

- The *Contractor* prepares forecasts of the final total of the Prices for the whole of the *service* at intervals no longer than **monthly.**

See GN on clause 20.5.

If Option C is used

- The *Contractor's share percentages* and the *share ranges* are

See GN on clause 53 before completing this section.

share range				Contractor's share percentage
less than		**80** %		**40** %
from	**80** % to	**90** %		**40** %
from	**90** % to	**110** %		**50** %
greater than		**110** %		**80** %

- The *Contractor*'s share is assessed on **one year after the service period then four weeks after the end of the service period**.

If Option C or E is used

- The *Contractor* prepares forecasts of Defined Cost for the *service* at intervals no longer than **5** .... weeks.

The frequency will in most cases coincide with the monthly cycle of assessments, monthly meetings, monthly reports etc., so a five week maximum is sensible.

See GNs on clause 50.6.

- The *exchange rates* are those published in .... on .... (date).

See GNs on Option X1.

If Option X1 is used

- The proportions used to calculate the Price Adjustment Factor are

0......	linked to the index for	....
0......		....
0......		....
0......		....
0......		....
0......		....
0......	non-adjustable	

———
1.00

- The *base date* for indices is ....

- The indices are those prepared by ....

See GNs on Option X3.

If Option X3 is used

- The *Employer* will pay for the items or activities listed below in the currencies stated

items and activities	other currency	total maximum payment in the currency
....	....	....
....	....	....
....	....	....
....	....	....

- The *exchange rates* are those published in ....
  on .... (date).

See GNs on Option X12.

If Option X12 is used

- The *Client* is

  Name ....

  Address ....

  ....

- The *Client*'s *objective* is

  ....

  ....

  ....

  ....

  ....

  ....

- The Partnering Information is in

....
....
....
....
....

See GNs on Option X13.

If Option X13 is used

- The amount of the performance bond is ....

See GNs on Option X17.

If Option X17 is used

- The *service level table* is in document **SLT1**.

See GNs on Option X18.

If Option X18 is used

- The *Contractor*'s liability to the *Employer* for indirect or consequential loss is limited to **$250,000 (two hundred and fifty thousand dollars)**.
- For any one event, the *Contractor*'s liability to the *Employer* for loss of or damage to the *Employer*'s property is limited to **$1,000,000 (one million dollars)**.
- The *Contractor*'s liability for Defects due to his design of an item of Equipment is **$100,000 (one hundred thousand dollars)**.
- The *Contractor*'s total liability to the *Employer* for all matters arising under or in connection with this contract, other than excluded matters, is limited to **$500,000 (five hundred thousand dollars)**.

- The *end of liability date* is **6** years after the end of the *service period*.

See GNs on Option X19.

If Option X19 is used

- The *Contractor* submits a Task Order programme to the *Service Manager* within **5** days of receiving the Task Order.

See GNs on Option X20.

If Option X20 is used (but not if Option X12 is also used)

- The *incentive schedule* for Key Performance Indicators is in document **IS1**.
- A report of performance against each Key Performance Indicator is provided at intervals of **3** months.

See GNs on Option Y(UK)1.

If Option Y(UK)1 is used and the *Employer* is to pay any charges made and is paid interest paid by the *project bank*

- The *Employer* is to pay any charges made and is paid interest paid by the *project bank*.

See GNs on Option Y(UK)3.

If Option Y(UK)3 is used

• term	person or organisation
....	....
....	....
....	....
....	....

The provision would be added if Y(NZ)2 is used.

If Option Y(NZ)2 is used

• term	person or organisation
....	....
....	....
....	....
....	....

If Option Y(UK)1 and Y(UK)3 are both used

• term	person or organisation
The provisions of Option Y(UK)1	Named Suppliers

If Option Z is used

- The *additional conditions of contract* are **in document reference ACoC1.**

The *additional conditions of contract* will become part of the contract, and so should be easily identified and logically located. Most people attach them to the Contract Data part one.

Part two – Data provided by the *Contractor*

Completion of the data in full, according to the Options chosen, is essential to create a complete contract.

Statements given in all contracts

- The *Contractor* is

Name	**FM Contracting Ltd**
Address	**The Hollow**
	Christchurch
	New Zealand
	Tel + 64 (03-321 3909).

Full legal name of Contractor.

Use the address from which the *Contractor* intends to manage the contract. This need not be the company's registered address.

- The *direct fee percentage* is **13%**.

See GNs on clause 11.2(8).

- The *subcontracted fee percentage* is **13%**.

See GNs on clause 11.2(8).

- The key people are

Frequently, the *Employer* will have listed in the Instructions to Tenderers the jobs for which he wants to see key people nominated.

See GNs on clause 24.1.

(1) Name **Mrs Smith**

Job **FM Manager**

Responsibilities **Manage the day to day running of the contract**

Qualifications **as attached CV**

Experience **as attached CV.**

(2) Name **Mr John Clean**

Job **Contracts Director**

Responsibilities **Overall responsibility for successful delivery of FM services on the contract**

Qualifications **as attached CV**

Experience **as attached CV.**

See GNs on clause 11.2(14).

- The following matters will be included in the Risk Register

Lack of local grounds maintenance expertise

Some catering requirements are seasonal

Short contract duration but considerable up-front investment required

Optional statements

The *Employer* should insert the appropriate optional statements for completion by tenderers before issuing the enquiry documents.

If the *Contractor* is to provide Service Information for his design

- The Service Information for the *Contractor*'s design is in ....

If a plan is identified in the Contract Data

- The plan identified in the Contract Data is

reference FM/Plan/1.

Tenderers to state reference to their priced *price list*.

See GNs on *price list*.

If Option A, C or E is used

- The *price list* is attached **PL1.**

If Option A or C is used

- The tendered total of the Prices is **$875,000 (eight hundred and seventy five thousand dollars).**

If the *Employer* has asked tenderers to insert this figure in the Form of Tender there may be no need to repeat it here.

See GNs on Option Y(UK)1.

If Option Y(UK)1 is used

- The *project bank* is used ....
- The *named suppliers* are ....